Healing Symbols from a Higher Dimension

Britta Hochkeppel

FISHER KING PUBLISHING

Healing Symbols from a Higher Dimension

Copyright © Britta Hochkeppel 2021

ISBN 978-1-913170-90-5

All rights reserved. No part of this publication may be reproduced or distributed in any form or by any means, or stored in a database or electronic retrieval system without the prior written permission of Fisher King Publishing Ltd.

The author of this book does not dispense medical advice nor prescribe the use of any technique as a form of treatment, either directly or indirectly.

The intention of the author is to offer information to help readers in their quest for physical wellbeing and good health.

Thank you for respecting the author of this work.

Published by
Fisher King Publishing
The Old Barn
York Road
Thirsk
YO7 3AD
England
www.fisherkingpublishing.co.uk

Dedication

This inspirational book has been co-written with guidance and information downloaded to me from more highly evolved dimensional light beings at this much needed time in our existence.

It has been transfered into my awareness as a gift for us all in order to introduce and translate their high vibrational frequency Healing Symbols that will contribute to raising the vibration of humanity at this much needed time.

The intention of this book is to manifest these powerful healing symbols into our physical world and bodies to support healing on a cellular level and to raise our vibration as a collective consciousness.

The unique frequencies of the healing symbols are recognised by our cells and transposed into healing vibrations that are absorbed by the entire mind-body system.

I dedicate this book to all the souls who are awake and seek to find healing, and who desire to gain a deeper insight into the truth of who they are and their true purpose.

Acknowledgements

I would like to thank all the souls who have contributed and inspired me on my journey to this day. To all that have touched my heart by seeking my guidance and for allowing me to contribute towards helping activate your self-healing memory.

My gratitude and love goes out to all of you who have taken part in my continuously evolving path as an Intuitive Healer and Holistic Light Worker.

By writing this book, my wish is to inspire all the awakened souls that are looking to raise their internal vibration and, as a result, to contribute towards raising the electromagnetic field on our planet as a collective conscious awareness.

Love

Biography

I was born in Germany, Schleswig-Holstein, a small quiet city near the Danish border where the Vikings used to come over once upon a time in 795. I am a born Intuitive Healer and became aware that I could sense the energy around me when I was six years old.

My grandmother was a Wart Charmer and very knowledgeable about herbs. She kept her gift a secret and never really spoke to me about it. She was very special. With her passing, my journey began as I focused on finding a way to get a sign from her or a reading.

My mother and I moved to England when I was twelve years old. I moved back to Germany at the age of seventeen to work as a Lithographer whilst living with my father and stepmother. From that time, I travelled back and forth and booked in to have readings with different Psychics in England whenever I could. I was fascinated by the afterlife and wanted to explore whether there was any truth in it. As well as learning more about the spirit, I did an intensive course for two and a half years at the University for Naturopathic Medicine alongside my job.

My quest has always been to find answers and explore the truth about who we are, why we are here, and what causes disease or pain. My own history of physical ailments and trauma added to my desire to find answers and solutions to ensure true healing can occur.

After being awarded my Diploma in Naturopathy, I moved to England in 2000. I continued my quest for learning by studying Progressive Kinesiology in 2004 and became a Reiki Master in 2009. I attended a Psychic College for one and a half years to enhance my abilities in 2008. I also practise Sound Healing, which is channelled, as well as my art and Psychic Surgery. It has been a non-stop evolving journey of learning.

I have developed my abilities to combine my Naturopathic medical knowledge with my gift to read and connect the energy body and the Auric Field. My clients are drawn to me for help from all over the UK, Europe and USA.

My first book, The Key To Loving Yourself, is a successful self-help book that gives people the ability to unlock their own emotional happiness. It is available to order from my website, www.vitaserena.co.uk

Since 2017, I have become increasingly aware of signs from beings of higher intelligence. This awareness has been further enhanced during recent months. In 2017, I was given the first set of 11 Healing Symbols to channel and download. During the lockdown of 2020, I channelled another 11 Healing Symbols. The connection I have with what I call the higher dimensions has increased, and I trust the messages and requests they give me.

The most recent request I received was to write this book,

Healing Symbols from a Higher Dimension, which was mostly channelled but also includes my perspective on things. The aim of the book is to inspire people and provide them with the key to the code and the practical symbols they need to raise their vibration. Only through the combined efforts of many individuals doing so can we raise our overall planetary vibration, too.

Britta Hochkeppel, 2020

Contents

Foreword		i
Chapter 1	How it all Began	1
Chapter 2	Light Language Symbols	6
Chapter 3	Healing Symbols from a Higher Dimension for the Light Body	9
Chapter 4	Frequency and Vibration of Emotions	40
Chapter 5	Emotional Chart Guide	48
Chapter 6	Healing Symbols from a Higher Dimension for the Physical Body	53
Chapter 7	Awareness	84
Chapter 8	Your Belief System is Your Healer	89
Chapter 9	How to Raise your Vibration	94
Chapter 10	Living in a Higher Vibrational State	115

Foreword

I have been practising as a Naturopath, Kinesiologist, Reiki Master and Energy/Intuitive Healer for the last 23 years. For me, it is normal to step into the Quantum Field with my left foot firmly planted in the physical reality of everyday life, while my right foot treads the enchanted world beyond space or time, as a shaman, mystic, visionary and Energy Healer.

I have long known about the healing powers of frequency but only in recent years have more people opened up to accept and allow themselves to speak about "energy". I have always observed the "global vibe" and flow with the concept of the Universe and the Quantum Field. I have sensed energy around me since early childhood and have been very lucky to encounter many unique and magical moments connected to a variety of energy beings.

In this book, I will unite and blend energy medicine with vibrational medicine downloaded shortly after recovering from what I now know was a type of Coronavirus, which I contracted in December 2017. These unique healing symbols help to raise the vibration in the energy body-system (our emotional body) and the physical body. I received these symbols from higher dimensional beings which contribute towards shining much needed light and healing on earth and its occupants.

Everything is Energy

We are beings of pure energy. We are composed of countless molecules flowing in a close formation, bringing us the physical experience that we have in our body and in this world; the unique and exquisite illusion we call our reality.

Looking at your hand, it appears solid. However, if it is magnified millions of times, you would come face to face with a single atom.

If magnified further, one would find nothing but empty space, however, you would witness energy currents zipping around at the speed of light.

Since the beginning of our existence, planet earth has been influenced by two types of energy force. The first type, negative and depleting energies, inspire and guide the types of human that resonate on a low vibration, who seek pleasure in creating an empire built on fear while ensuring the masses stay suppressed.

Then we have the positive and higher vibrational state energies, who always help or support others as well as facing their own path of evolution, thereby raising their vibration.

Now in the year 2021, I ask, "What has changed?"

Out of Balance

In my opinion, the negative and depleting energies are still manipulating and inspiring corrupt business people and selected organisations to continue with maintaining mass control.

They are feverishly plotting to keep the masses suppressed, using negative brainwashing techniques via the media; fabricating man-made viruses which are killing thousands of innocent people and introducing new and even more health-damaging frequencies such as the introduction of 5G. This is incompatible with health as it penetrates the cellular membrane and adversely impacts a variety of our biological processes. The people with knowledge and awareness are kept suppressed and accused of heresy, whilst the real lies continue to be sold to the masses as truth.

The installation of thousands of WiFi connections in schools and workplaces as well as conveniently erecting 5G masts around the country continued during lockdown, while innocent people were dying or frozen with fear. Huge numbers of satellites (estimated to be 53,000 or more by 2027) are planned to be launched to orbit the Earth, which unless stopped will blast an even higher life-depleting radiation onto the planet. This has all been happening right under our noses during lockdown without anyone's consent, while the people with knowledge have been forcibly delayed in their ability to take action against it. We, our children, and the animals on this planet will not survive the consequences of this devastating and depleting frequency if their plans are realised.

I hope that the positive, collective consciousness will unite in time and ensure that we ascend into the golden age.

Currently, it appears that the masses are stuck in an energetic state of fear and uncertainty. This provides an ideal opportunity for the seeds of lies to be sown in order to uphold the illusion of offering help which, in reality, is just another version of mass control. I believe that this has been put into place to ensure mass control on an even larger scale, so that the average human can continue to serve as "energetic cattle".

A New Vibrational State

Amongst all of this, we are moving from the third dimension of consciousness into a higher vibrational state. In the third dimension, our current vibration, we experience lower vibrational states such as selfishness, violence, greed and competition. As we move into a higher vibrational state, the fifth dimension, we experience vibrations of unity-consciousness, compassion and unconditional love that will become the dominant emotions.

This energy shift on a global scale makes it much more difficult for negative and depleting energies to maintain their power, which is one of the reasons why they are trying their utmost to prevent our awareness and knowledge from awakening. So, for a while, we will experience the clash of these two opposing energetic forces; the higher vibrational state against the negative influencers.

The reason why I feel that now is the right time to introduce the higher dimensional healing symbols is that they will help us through this time of transformation and uncertainty.

The Power of Symbols

Symbols date back to ancient history, long before language was created. When we talk about the study of symbols today, there are different kinds of symbols that we have become accustomed to, sometimes without even thinking about it. Symbols represent a form of language that has no words and no sounds. I am fascinated by this form because it may represent one of the most advanced and sophisticated forms of communication called an ideogram.

An ideogram does precisely what it suggests. It is the symbol that represents an entire idea or an entire concept without ever uttering a word, phrase or sound to describe that idea and without needing the alphabet.

Each of my downloaded symbols own a signature vibration which represents the concept of healing, recalibrating and raising your internal vibration as a living energy system. The chapters that follow will introduce you to these symbols and explain how we can use them to raise your vibration, individually as well as collectively.

Stepping forward as a messenger, I am aware that introducing something new such as these vibrational healing symbols will divide opinion, but I can only follow my heart and my truth. May the healing vibration of the high dimensional symbols benefit everyone who comes into contact with them and raise the vibrational state within their emotional, mental and physical body around the world.

Chapter 1

How it all Began

It started in February 2018, not long after my recovery from a virus. We were experiencing heavy snowfall. Most shops in the village were closed except for a local café, so my mother and I arranged to meet there for a cup of tea. However, upon our arrival, we noticed that there was only one lady working. It transpired that due to the weather conditions, she was the only member of staff that had made it to work that day and was struggling to serve all the customers on her own.

I offered my assistance and ended up helping her for about an hour or so. I took customer orders, served them and helped to tidy up. I found myself enjoying the spontaneous shift from being a customer to a waitress. After two hours we left as it had all quietened down. I walked my mother home, who also lives in the village, before making my way back to my house.

As I arrived at the top of my lane, I saw a group of teenagers in distress. As I walked closer, one came towards me and told me that my 15 year old neighbour had lost her mobile phone in the nearby field. She was very upset about the situation, so I offered to join in and help search for it. The snow was deep, and after 45 minutes, all we could see were the trampled footsteps we had left behind. It was getting dark and everyone was cold. Just as we were about to give up the search, I heard the euphoric cry from one of the girls confirming that she had found it.

I was glad to be able to return to my warm home and enjoy a hot cup of tea. I smiled to myself, reflecting on all the excitement I had experienced in one day in our little village, and how I had enjoyed being able to support others in need of help. I knew that my clients would not be able to attend their appointments and surrendered to the circumstances.

A little while later, my partner arrived after his day at work and kindly dropped off some food for me. His workplace was closer to the bigger supermarkets where the roads were slightly better. After he delivered the food, he and I exchanged conversation about my adventures of the day until his attention was grabbed by something he noticed on the bonnet of my car parked directly outside my house.

As he drew my awareness towards it, I noticed a strange pattern marked in the snow. My initial reaction was to ask if he had created it himself, but he assured me he had not. I soon realised that he could not have done so as there were absolutely no footsteps in the snow around my car, suggesting that it could only have been created from above. I quickly reached for my tablet and took a couple of photographs while staring in wonder at this most peculiar and intriguing design.

Healing Symbols from a Higher Dimension

Image 1: Photo view from above the bonnet.

Image 2: View from the side of the bonnet.

After a brief period, I began to wonder if this unusual pattern could have been a rough landing created by a bird, which could have then fluttered its wings to gather momentum to take off again. However, after closer inspection and zooming in on the images, it was clear to me that this could not possibly have been created by a bird, not least because of the absence of bird footprints, but also the overall body shape and razor-sharp lines. This was not the result of a bird landing on my car bonnet. It appeared to be a sign, but from who and why?

I had experienced many encounters with energies in the past. Still, I had never received a physical sign like this one on my car's bonnet, right in front of my kitchen window. I had not moved or touched my car, and there had been no other people around. If there had been someone, they would have had to enter through my gates, which I would have heard as I live in a very quiet area. Also, the thick blanket of snow would have highlighted any footprints. I had an inner knowing that this was some form of a sign, so I started researching to try to discover the meanings of signs or symbols.

My research gave insight into images of ancient writings but nothing looked similar. I am very familiar with symbolism dating back to Ancient Egypt and the Mayan civilisations, as well as Viking and Celtic symbols and ancient written words.

Symbols were used as the building blocks of early human language and were also used as a portal for humans to communicate with the world of the Gods. The design and meaning of the symbols would very much depend on historical background, location, and specific religions and Gods worshipped. None showed any resemblance to mine. This image was much more intricate in detail. It was somehow made unique by combining the feather-light whips in contrast to the razor-sharp edges in the front and the depth of it, all created in the freshly fallen snow.

I decided to meditate on my findings over the coming days and to explore whether I might receive further insight, as in the past I had always received clarity and answers to any question I had. The following morning, I sat in meditation and the immediate answer was: "A new guide is entering your energy and will download healing symbols to assist the frequency shift." I have learnt to trust the information and that was all I received on that day.

A few nights passed. Then, after about a week and for a period of three days, I woke at 3 a.m. each morning receiving symbols which were given to me at such a speed that I found it hard to keep up. Initially, I scribbled them all into a journal but was told a few days later that I would have to create artwork in order to present these symbols in a specific format, as they needed to be seen.

Chapter 2

Light Language Symbols

Light language is information channelled from other beings in other realms or star systems. I would add to this by stating that the information originates from beings with a higher vibration and awareness and comes with light, meaning its healing qualities are extremely pure.

The higher dimensional healing symbols access the subconscious where deep healing can occur. The vibration is received by the cellular system, similar to sound, and bypasses the intellect, which means it travels straight to the core of the cellular disorder. The symbols create cellular order where cellular chaos is present.

The symbols are divided into two categories:

1. Healing and raising the vibration of the energy-body, i.e. the emotional body.

2. Healing and raising the vibration of the physical body.

The recipient will receive the healing vibration code in two ways:

1. Looking at the chosen healing symbol, the healing frequency will be received by the retina-brain-heart

connection and then absorbed and transposed by the cellular system.

2. Chanting the name of the chosen healing symbol whilst gazing at the symbol and practising a deeper breath amplifies the intensity of the frequency, which in turn enhances the healing.

Energy healing begins instantly. It is our intellectual dependence on our belief system that creates resistance, which we have often been conditioned with since childhood. The beauty of these higher dimensional healing symbols is that, although they appear simple, the origin of their vibrational code and the level of their vibrational power stems from the higher dimensions.

In time, the recipient will experience healing and the ability to maintain the raised vibration. This will give the individual the opportunity to change his or her way of thinking. Eventually, higher vibrational thoughts, feelings, and behaviours will manifest a shift in the electromagnetic field within the recipient's energy and physical body.

Thoughts and feelings generate a signature vibration which cannot be contained by the brain and is therefore transmitted into the surrounding energy field, otherwise known as the Quantum Field.

The higher dimensional Healing Symbols have been gifted to me to assist with raising the vibration of those of us who are suffering with a multitude of symptoms resulting from negative emotions. These have stagnated and manifested in anatomical sites of the physical body, or in the energy/emotional body, causing pain and/or preventing us from living a happy and fulfilling life.

The higher dimensional Healing Symbols vibrate at a very high frequency and activate our innate self-healing mechanisms by combining the power of the mind and the power of intention with deep breathing.

What I find so inspiring is the simplicity of this healing technique. To focus on a chosen symbol whilst chanting the name provided, enhanced with a conscious deep breathing method, appears so simple. Yet it is the beginning of a hugely complex healing process. The concept works on a similar level to working with the use of Sound Healing.

Vibrational healing works on the basis of "entrainment", which means that a higher frequency will influence or even nullify vibrations that resonate on a lower frequency, depleting negative thoughts and emotions.

Similar to Sound Healing, the vibration of the symbols bypass the interference of our often resistant intellectual brain and are then able to penetrate the cellular system, thereby initiating and supporting true healing changes.

The Healing Symbols have been created to raise the vibrational state within us and the electromagnetic field of the planet by using collective consciousness energy healing. The higher the number of individuals vibrating on a higher frequency, the more powerful the collective result.

Chapter 3

Healing Symbols from a Higher Dimension for the Light Body

The Healing Symbols from a higher dimension restore cellular order within our energy body and our physical body. Each symbol has its signature vibration and light language codename, and targets one or several areas within the energy body.

The recipient is asked to gaze at the chosen symbol for eight minutes, two to three times a day for 21 consecutive days. Whilst looking at the symbol, the recipient should be mindful of how they breathe, adopting a deeper and more conscious breath using the technique below.

Inhale deeply through the nose for four seconds, feeling it all the way down into your abdomen. Hold that breath for a further four seconds and then exhale slowly through the mouth for four to five seconds.

As you become more familiar with this deep breathing method, you will not only find yourself able to inhale and hold larger volumes of air, but you will also gain the ability to hold and exhale it over longer periods of time.

Counting as you breathe in before holding and then breathing out should only be used as a mental guideline, specifically for those who are new to this type of controlled breathing. You will need to remember to direct your main focus toward chanting the name of the symbol at the same time as using the deep and relaxed breathing method.

The name of the chosen symbol should be chanted in two parts, either in your mind or out loud, with every breath as follows.

As you inhale, say the first half of the name and as you exhale the second half. Repeat this rhythmically and slowly according to the timing of the breaths as you gaze at the symbol.

It is important to follow this ritual to assist in releasing old emotional patterns and to allow the new internal vibration to be processed by the mind-body system.

Symbol Name: Ra-Ha-Zi

The Eye of the Sun / Precious Soul of Light

This Healing Symbol radiates pure white light and brings instant illumination into any areas of darkness.

Replenishing and Stimulating the Pineal Gland

The pineal gland holds a very special position within our mind-body system. Its location is in the centre of the brain and it is often referred to as the "third eye". The pineal gland produces melatonin, which helps maintain the circadian rhythm and regulates reproductive hormones.

The pineal gland is sensitive to light and vibration. Studies have shown that it monitors magnetic fields and assists with orienting the body in space, acting as a navigation centre. This also explains why geomagnetic storms or environmental stress can affect it, leading to a variety of symptoms.

With higher exposure to ever-increasing levels of harmful electromagnetic radiation alongside the consumption of polluted drinking water high in fluoride, heavy metals, pesticides and pharmaceuticals, it is almost impossible to avoid experiencing imbalances of the pineal gland. These imbalances can lead to shrinkage and calcification, which in turn prevent the gland from functioning properly. We therefore have to find ways to enhance the inner light vibration of the cellular system in the pineal gland.

This Healing Symbol introduces the purest white light energy from the highest dimension and vibrates on an extraordinarily high frequency, helping to lift our energy.

It is ideal for all of those who suffer with:

- Depression
- Post Traumatic Stress Disorder (PTSD)
- Grief
- Hormonal disorders
- Menopause
- Post-Natal Depression
- Seasonal Adjustment Disorder (SAD)
- Lethargy
- Exhaustion
- Burnout

Chanted name sounds like: Ra Ha Zee

On the in breath: Ra Ha

On the out breath: Zee

Symbol Name: Ram-Ra

Balancer - Synchronises the left and right sides of the brain

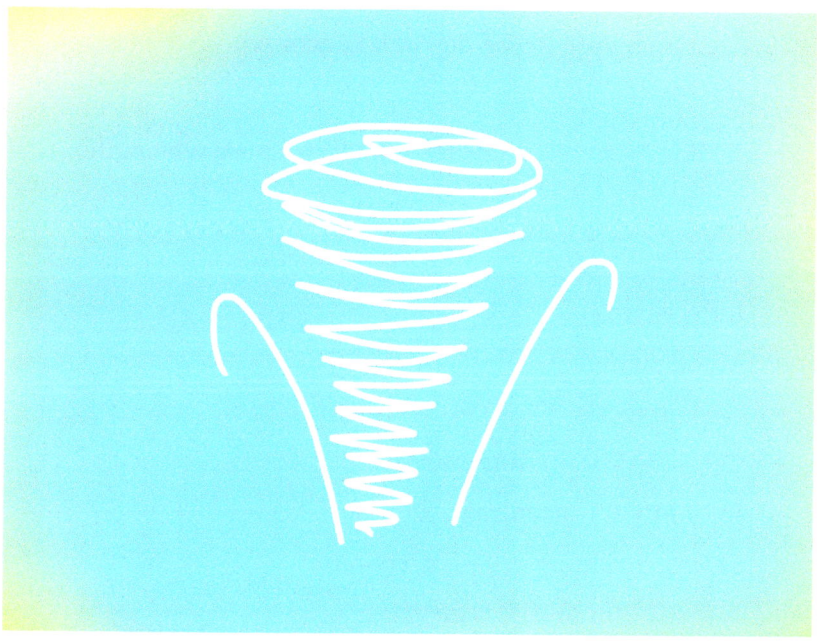

The left hemisphere of the brain connects more with linear thinking and mathematical, practical and analytical situations, whereas the right hemisphere of the brain is connected with the frequency of creative thinking and intuition, while being more focused on visual cues.

- Left brain: logical, objective, strategic, organisational, analytical, mathematical, detail orientated, reality based, written language, spoken language.

- Right brain: intuitive, imaginative, artistic, feeling, symbols and images, philosophical, appreciation of life, huge potential, adventurous, spiritual.

Stress and modern lifestyle as well as practising a low vibrational inner dialogue will deplete both hemispheres of the brain and contribute to various imbalances within the energy body system.

This Healing Symbol will bring balance to those who suffer with:

- Inability to focus
- Indecisiveness
- Mood swings
- Lack of focus
- One sided brain dominance
- Inability to concentrate
- Overactive inner criticism chatter
- Negative inner dialogue
- Overactive sympathetic nervous system
- Anxiety
- Mental stress

Chanted name sounds like: Rumrah

On the in breath: Rum

On the out breath: Rah

Symbol Name: Kura-Pakka

Protection

This Healing Symbol brings warmth and protection into your solar plexus energy body. The solar plexus has a central location where the thoracic rib cage meets the upper stomach region. Due to its location, it manages many of the organs surrounding it. These organs hold the quality of vibration we give them with the way we think and feel and what we choose to eat and drink.

Emotional issues and behaviours from a blocked solar plexus will result in a sense of low confidence and self-esteem issues. Everything is connected, so we need to make sure that we keep the vibration balanced and strong in our solar plexus energy centre, ensuring the balanced functioning of the surrounding organs.

The healing properties of this symbol include:

- Reduction in the sense of vulnerability and insecurity for those who are experiencing a period of transformation.
- Protection against darker energies, which can sometimes become more interested in you when you are growing your light, or where you are in contact with low vibrational beings on a regular basis who tend to either dump their psychic waste on you or drain your energy body.
- Protection for Light Workers and Healers.
- Nurtures and warms the solar plexus energy centre.
- Supports the energy function of the spleen, pancreas, stomach, gallbladder and liver by raising the vibrational frequency of the organs.

Chanted name sounds like: Kura Pakka

On the in breath: Kura

On the out breath: Pakka

Symbol Name: Assa

Expanded Awareness

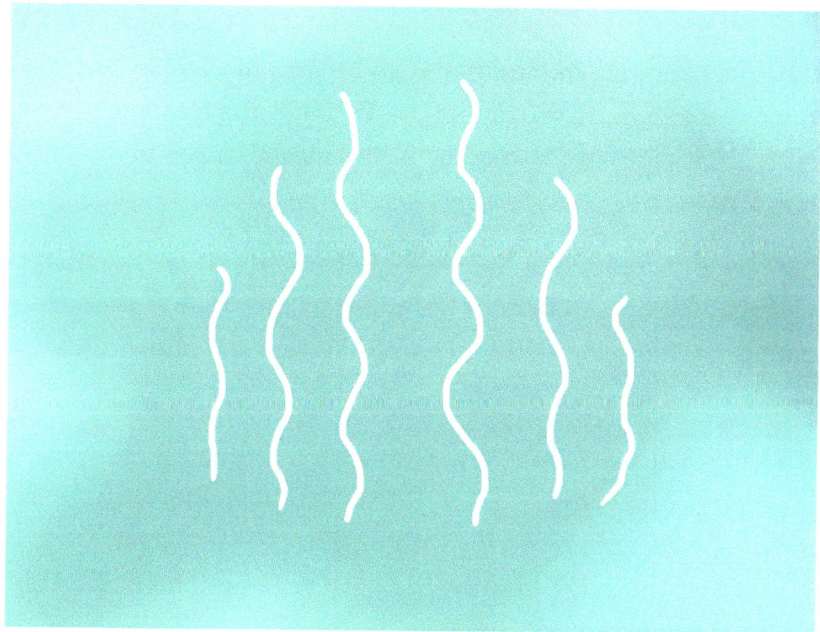

This Healing Symbol opens pathways to allow the ascending energy to flow upwards. It helps to stimulate the subtle energy pathways called "meridians". Meridians are a fine network of energy channels that connect the surface of the body with the internal organs. Every organ and major region in the body needs energy to flow in order to function.

The 12 meridians are the primary meridians through which Qi (Chi) flows. Each meridian terminates in an arm or a leg, and all have Yin and Yang properties. There are six meridians that are located in the inner region of the arms, legs, chest and torso.

The theory and practice of acupuncture originated in China around 6000 BC. To this day, acupuncture needles are used in specific energy points from the hundreds that exist to rebalance the energy flow within the meridians.

The flow of energy in meridians can become blocked externally by excessive cold, wind, dampness, dryness, fire (heat) or injury. Blockages can also occur from internal causes by emotions such as anger, sadness, fear, stress or depression.

The healing vibration of the Assa symbol frees the energy that has become stagnant by past traumatic events or unexpressed emotions within the meridian energy system and allows Qi to flow better.

In addition, it also helps those who wish to expand their knowledge or awareness about the truth of who they are, or those wishing to move forward or change their career, relationship, or living location but have been hesitant or fearful to take the next step.

- Supports the water element within the mind-body system
- Strengthens the fearful and insecure
- Strengthens the nervous system
- Supports and strengthens the kidney and bladder energy

This symbol helps with the release of the emotional vibrations:

- Anger
- Fear
- Insecurity

- Sadness

Chanted name sounds like: Ussa

On the in breath: Uss

On the out breath: Sah

Symbol Name: Fen-Ne

Enlightened Mind

This Healing Symbol raises the vibration of the brain energy. When your brain cells send signals, they release neurotransmitters; the "happy hormones" such as oxytocin, endorphins, dopamine and serotonin.

Oxytocin – is released during intimacy and strengthens relationships. It acts like a glue that binds healthy relationships together and helps to create trust. Mothers release oxytocin during childbirth and when breastfeeding. Oxytocin is the "cuddle" hormone and there are many ways to stimulate the release of this wonderful happy hormone.

Endorphins – are released in response to pain and stress and help to alleviate anxiety. They act as sedatives, diminishing your perception of pain. Along with exercise, laughter is one of the easiest ways to increase the level of endorphins. Aromatherapy and the smell of vanilla and lavender (or anything you recognise as a pleasant smell) will cause the brain to release endorphins.

Dopamine – motivates you to take action towards a goal and gives a surge of reinforced pleasure when achieving them.

Serotonin – is released when you feel significant or important and aware of your purpose. Specific foods also help the brain to release serotonin, such as dark green leafy vegetables, chia seeds and pumpkin seeds to name a few.

Depleting emotional vibrations slow down or block the release of these brain chemicals and can create a multitude of imbalances. The brain cannot tell the difference between a real event or an event created purely through thought alone and will release the same levels of hormones including stress hormones depending on the triggers.

This Healing Symbol helps with the release of negative emotional vibrations:

- Sadness
- Loneliness
- Depression
- Anxiety

- Stress

In addition, this healing frequency helps open the third eye (pineal gland) and:

- Allows creativity to flow
- Gives insight
- Offers solutions/answers
- Enhances positivity
- Is uplifting
- Balances brain chemicals
- Enhances the release of happy hormones

Chanted name sounds like: Fen Neh

On the in breath: Fen

On the out breath: Neh

Symbol Name: Ra-Hum

Cradled Inner Child

This Healing Symbol offers deep healing to the "wounded" inner child. It helps to soothe the soul when it requires assistance in the recovery from past trauma or abuse of any kind.

From the moment we begin our life's journey, we can experience a traumatic event or an entire chain of events which can become trapped in any anatomical site or layer of the energy-mind system.

Most unresolved emotional and physical trauma can lead to PTSD. These events include:

- Physical or sexual assault
- Abuse, including childhood or domestic abuse
- Serious health problems
- Childbirth experiences, such as losing a baby
- Sudden loss
- Sudden separation
- Exposure to traumatic events at work

Having been exposed to trauma and suffering, the emotional scars can lead to many low emotional vibrations.

This Healing Symbol helps with the release of the emotional vibrations of feeling:

- Lack of self-love
- Unloved
- Despondent
- Disconnected
- Loneliness
- Sadness

In addition, this symbol helps with the healing process of a broken heart and releases a gentle, soothing and nurturing vibration into the heart centre.

Chanted name sounds like: Raah-Humm

On the in breath: Raah

On the out breath: Humm

Symbol Name: Sattidee
Peace for the Soul

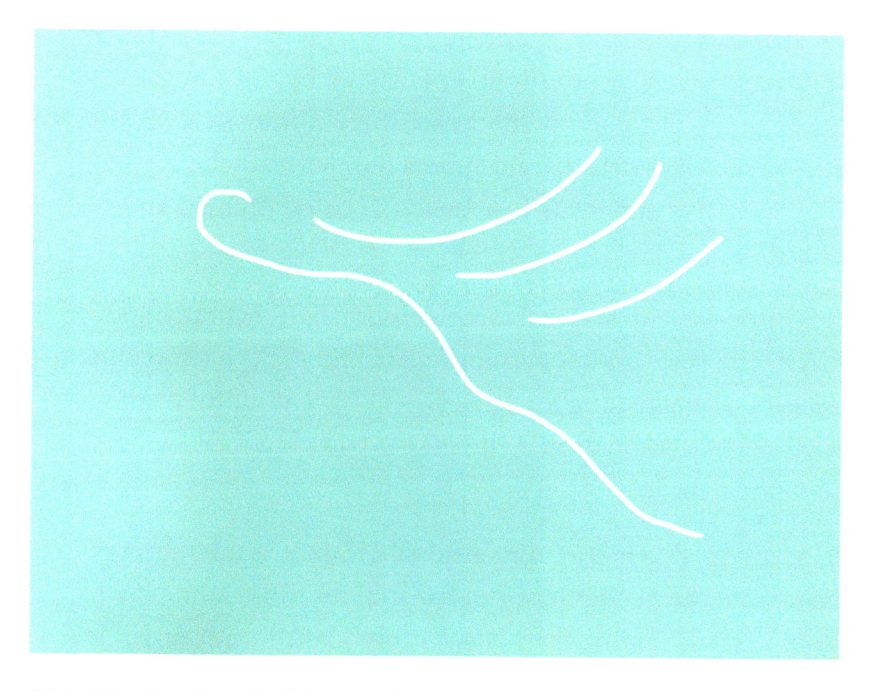

This Healing Symbol brings the vibration of peace into the spirit energy emotional body. The healing quality of this vibration stimulates the parasympathetic nervous system.

The parasympathetic nervous system is one of two divisions of the autonomic nervous system. It promotes peristalsis (the waves of smooth muscle contraction that move food through the intestine) and the process of digestion. The parasympathetic system also promotes the secretion of different glands and decreases respiration and heart rate. It is essential that the function of this system stays in balance with the opposing system, the sympathetic nervous system.

When we experience constant mental levels of stress and anxiety, most of us suffer with an "over-stimulated" sympathetic nervous system, which suppresses the healthy function of the parasympathetic system. Living in a constant state of stress ("fight or flight") registered by the amygdala in our brain, our body will release stress hormones such as adrenaline and cortisol, which puts our sympathetic system into overdrive and leads to a feeling of being drained and unwell.

It is impossible to stay balanced emotionally, mentally and physically if we do not become aware and make a conscious decision to make time for ourselves to have mindful breaks, such as meditation or deep breathing techniques and other soothing exercises.

In addition, this higher dimensional Healing Symbol brings peace into the deeper levels of the soul for those who may be close to transitioning from this earthly plane into another. It helps to ease the one who is transitioning to a higher level. It assists with peaceful insight and enhances the understanding of lessons learnt, restoring peace and helping to ease suffering.

This Healing Symbol helps with the release of negative emotional vibrations by:

- Helping to release the signature vibration of anger
- Helping to release the signature vibration of resentment
- Helping to release the signature vibration of pride
- Helping to liberate from the chains of the ego

Chanted name sounds like: Sat-tee-deh

On the in breath: Sat-tee

On the out breath: Deh

Symbol Name: Ra-Mi

The Energiser

This Healing Symbol accelerates and stimulates the vibration of joy and vitality, warming the solar plexus and heart centres. It can be used when we need an inner smile or to be uplifted and to raise our vibrational state. It is the "energetic espresso", where the energy surge is instant and penetrates deep into the entire mind-body energy system.

This Healing Symbol nurtures and balances the adrenals. It helps to loosen rigid thought patterns and invites us to reconnect with our ability to be playful. As well as warming the solar plexus and heart centres, it activates the digestive process and helps to speed up the metabolism.

The adrenals are two small glands that sit on top of the kidneys and produce several hormones, including cortisol. When we are under stress, we produce and release short bursts of cortisol into our blood stream. If we are exposed to prolonged periods of stress, the adrenals can become fatigued. We can create the same level of stress just by thinking negative thoughts or through the practice of constant negative inner dialogue. Remember, every emotion and feeling impacts the entire energy-body system.

Adrenal fatigue can cause symptoms such as:

- Brain fog
- Depressive moods
- Low energy levels
- Salt and sweet cravings
- Light-headedness
- Feeling shaky
- Feeling lethargic
- Burnout syndrome

The healing vibration of this symbol helps with the release of:

- Sadness
- Despair
- Negative inner dialogue
- Constant criticism
- Low self-esteem
- Low self-worth
- Rigid thought systems

- Feeling stuck
- Taking life too seriously
- Imbalances based around giving and receiving
- Mental exhaustion

Chanted name sounds like: Raah-Mee

On the in breath: Raah

On the out breath: Mee

Symbol Name: So-Tis

Empowerment and Alignment

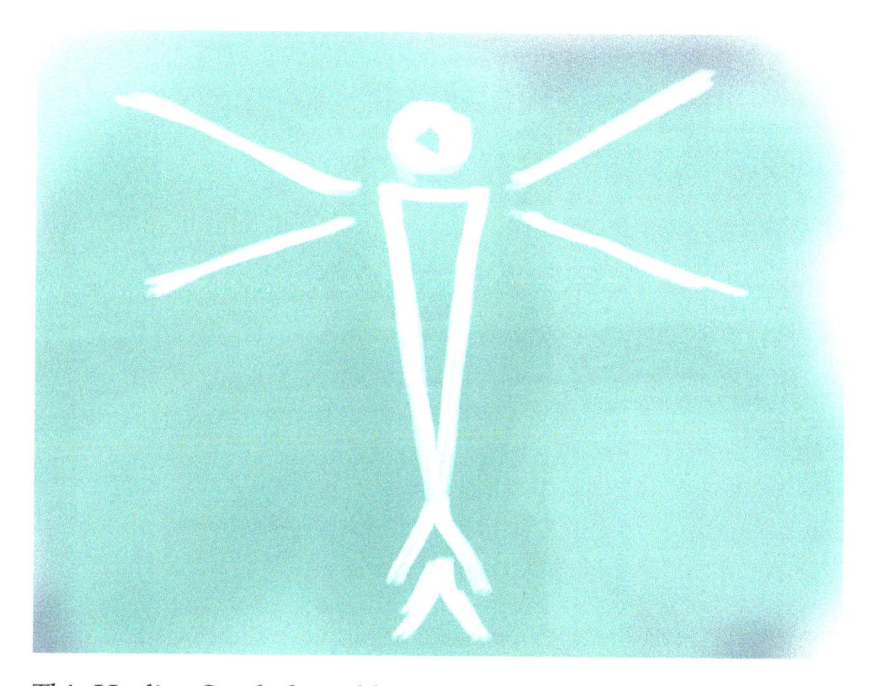

This Healing Symbol recalibrates the Auric Field energy layers and offers protection and grounding. It provides guidance and healthy boundaries for those who "travel", physically, mentally, or energetically, including:

- Astral travel (out of body experience)
- Meditation
- Airline travel (jet lag)

This higher dimensional Healing Symbol anchors the subtle energies during the journeys of the energy body and helps to keep it safe. It supports alignment of the Auric Field layers. The colours and vibrations of the Auric Field can be seen by people who are born Sensitive or Intuitive. Healers see them too.

Maintaining a strong Auric Field is important for our physical health. Releasing emotional baggage helps to correct tears and holes or disturbances within this field.

The Auric Field consists of several layers:

The Etheric layer – closest to the physical body and is connected to the base or root chakra of our energy system.

The Emotional layer – extends one to three inches from the physical body and is connected to the sacral chakra of our energy system.

The Mental layer – sits directly outside the emotional body extending three to eight inches from the physical body and is connected to the solar plexus chakra.

The Astral layer –bridges between the lower vibrations and the higher vibrations of the spiritual body. It extends about twelve inches and is connected to the heart chakra.

The Etheric template –extends out about two feet and is the blueprint of the physical body and is connected to the throat chakra.

The Celestial/Causal layer – extends up to two and a half feet and is connected to the third eye chakra.

The Spiritual layer – can extend up to three feet and is connected to the crown chakra and protects all the other chakras.

The healing vibration of this Healing Symbol helps to:

- Recalibrate those who feel out of alignment
- Protect and ground energy for Healers and Sensitives
- Realign the Auric Field layers of those who spend a lot of their time travelling
- Empower the inner being
- Calm and realign the entire energy body network
- Strengthen the nervous system

Chanted name sounds like: Sow-Tiss

On the in breath: Sow

On the out breath: Tiss

Symbol Name: Sa-Fi
Manifesting

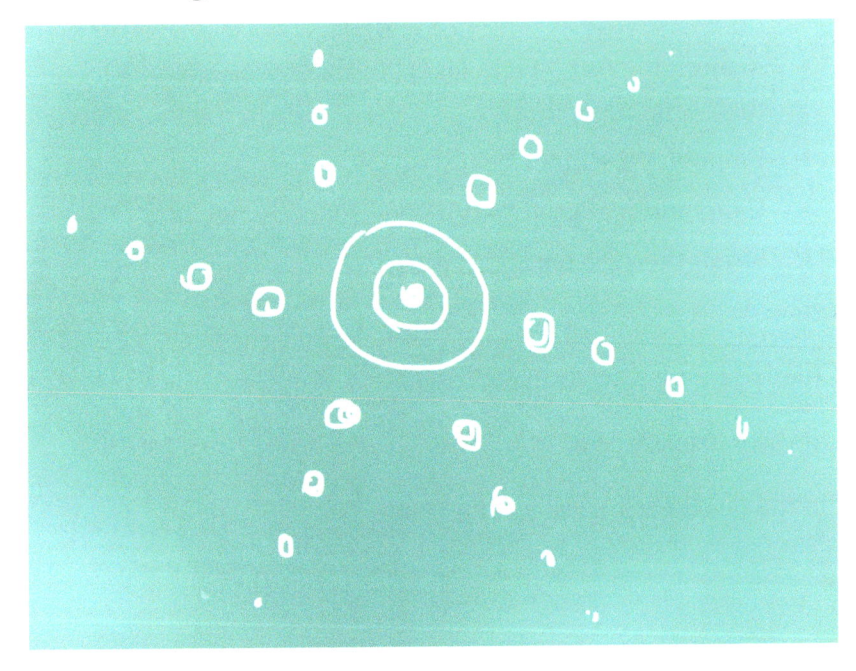

This Healing Symbol supports us if we are practising the law of attraction, which follows the law of vibration. We create matter from energy. Before we can begin to manifest what we truly desire, we need to learn to understand how it works and what we as the "sender" wish to draw into our reality.

We need to vibrate on the same energy that we wish to attract back to us.

For example, if we wish to attract the ideal partner into our lives who is confident, generous, gentle and loving, we must be all that we seek.

If we are selfish, lacking in confidence and judgemental, it is likely we will attract a partner that is selfish, lacking in confidence and judgemental.

We can attract different types of partner into our lives at different times depending on the traits we are displaying at any particular time. We have to let go of any resistance blocking our ability to attract the right people.

It is not the repetition of positive affirmations that bring what we desire closer, but the vibration of the affirmations which our mind-body system understands and emanates out into the Quantum Field.

In order for vibration to manifest into matter, we need to:

- Be aware of our resistant thoughts and negative beliefs and release them
- Give ourselves permission to receive
- Do our best to keep our vibrations high
- Be clear about what we want
- Take inspired action
- Use effective tools which help us to keep our vibration high

The healing vibration of this symbol:

- Draws what we desire closer into our energy
- Supports positive transformation
- Enhances courage
- Manifests new ideas

- Enhances confidence
- Strengthens the throat chakra
- Helps with expressing truth

Chanted name sounds like: Zar-Fee

On the in breath: Zar

On the out breath: Fee

Symbol Name: Da-Va

Peaceful Insight

This Healing Symbol creates an energetic link between your mind and your inner being (higher intelligence). Our inner being is connected to the non-physical realm of consciousness.

Imagination is the mode of communication between the mind and the inner being. You can say that your inner being is connected to the non-physical realm of consciousness and the wholeness of it. Your mind is observing the physical reality and is thus a translator of the physical realm. A seamless communication between your mind and your inner being ensures a harmonious physical expression. Our inner being enjoys the view that our mind gives it, and our mind needs the guidance and intelligence of the inner being.

Most of us have experienced periods of time where our communication and trust with our inner being has become disconnected. This can result in making the same mistakes or recreating the same life lessons over and over. Another reason why we can lack trust or are unable to hear our inner voice stems from us being conditioned to deny its existence from an early age. By learning that we are limited beings and that imagination or intuition is nothing more than an imaginary toy during childhood, we are taught that it should not be listened to.

Prolonged exposure to stress, anxiety, living an unhealthy lifestyle and thinking low vibrational thoughts will suppress the communication of our mind with our inner being and vice versa. It is therefore of great importance to make time to reconnect with your inner being. Meditation is a great tool to explore our inner world and to communicate with our inner being.

The healing vibration of this symbol helps with the release of:

- Feeling disconnected
- Insecurity
- Indecisiveness
- Confusion
- Stress
- Irritation
- Restlessness

Da-Va can also be seen as the "comfort blanket" for the emotional body and can:

- Soothe and calm the entire energy system
- Heal and nurture the heart energy centre
- Help with hearing the wisdom of the higher self
- Enhance awareness
- Help hidden potential to emerge
- Help with creating a better quality relationship with oneself

Chanted name sounds like: Dar-Vah

On the in breath: Dar

On the out breath: Vah

Chapter 4

Frequency and Vibration of Emotions

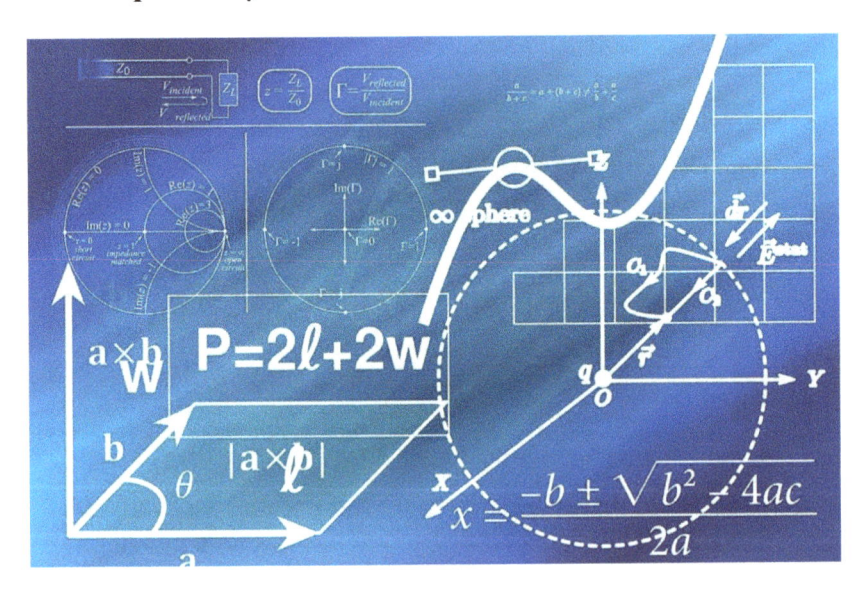

Frequency

Heinrich Rudolf Hertz (22 February 1857 – 1 January 1894) was a German physicist who conclusively proved the existence of electromagnetic waves, as predicted by James Clerk Maxwell's equations of electromagnetism. The unit of frequency, or cycle per second, was named "hertz" in his honour. One hertz (Hz) is one cycle per second.

We each resonate as a huge vessel of vibrating particles,

constantly giving off and sending out electromagnetic waves into the Quantum Field, and each one of us vibrates at a signature frequency. The higher the vibration or frequency of our energy, the lighter we feel in our physical, emotional and mental body.

A high frequency in the body results in better health. It has been shown that positive emotions raise all physical functions. The higher the frequency, the more DNA is stimulated and everything flows at a healthy pace. It has been shown that a normal healthy body has a frequency of 62-72 Hz. However, if the body drops below this frequency, we begin to suffer from illness and disease.

Emotion means energy movement. Energy is in constant motion and each emotion has its own frequency. The amplitude depends on the quality of our thoughts at the frequency they generate. Every emotion molecule has its own signature vibrational energy and therefore frequency. Emotions can lodge anywhere in our body. The size of the area they influence can vary from a tiny cluster of cells to a big formation.

With us being an energy body, negative emotions held over time will damage and attack healthy tissue. Negative emotions are created by negative thoughts and belief systems, as a result of trauma experienced in our past that creates chaos at an atomic level.

Atomic chaos leads to chaos on the molecular level, which in turn leads to chaos at the cellular level. When enough cells are in a state of chaos or "cellular stress", we feel it as a sign of discomfort, dysfunction or other physical ailment in our body.

Negative and depleting emotions vibrate on a lower frequency and prevent us from manifesting and attracting positive changes into our mind-body system. If we have negative, low vibrational thoughts, emotions and behaviours, we generate a low frequency which in time will result in imbalances of the physical body.

The emotional frequencies in hertz below are approximate frequencies only and can differ slightly according to different causes of the emotion.

Low Wavelength Frequency Emotions

- Grief: 20 Hz
- Shame: 25 Hz
- Guilt: 30 Hz
- Fear: 19 Hz
- Anger: 28 Hz

Compare these with the higher wavelength vibrations below that are generated by positive emotions and feelings.

High Wavelength Frequency Emotions

- Happiness: 400 Hz
- Joy: 540 Hz
- Peace: 590 Hz
- Love: 700-780 Hz

The physical body is the vessel of our subconscious mind which stores our behaviours and past experiences. From the very beginning of our life we start to encode our experiences, both good and bad. Our subconscious mind stores these recordings of the past and makes them real to our conscious mind later in life.

Emotions naturally accumulate. We tend to suppress or push our unwanted emotions away because we have been taught to ignore or suppress emotions that do not feel good to us. Once negative molecules of emotion have formed, they are real. You will be unable to remove them from the body unless you commit to connecting with yourself and your emotions and feelings, and to finding ways to release them.

Negative emotions are stored in anatomical sites, which unfortunately means our bodies store billions of emotional molecules. Depending on their vibration, they can affect both the physicality and function of the organs, which will very often lead to disease and illness. Negative emotional molecules become lodged due to our subconscious mind holding onto the data frequency because we are either unaware or disconnected from our inner mind and body. This will be enhanced by a negative belief system which runs on the subconscious autopilot program in our physical body and nervous system.

It is important that we learn how to connect with our subconscious mind and emotions and learn how to release the negative and unhelpful ones. We need to obtain insight into how to replace old emotions with new, positive or higher vibrational thoughts and emotions.

Every so-called problem within your body is a portal. It is your doorway and opportunity to access this invisible, unseen energy that is guiding our cells to communicate from our heart-brain to our body and from our body into the outside world.

If your body presents you with a physical pain, look at your symptom as a sign and an opportunity to allow old and outworn patterns to surface and be replaced. Nothing in your body hurts without being correlated to an emotion you have experienced in the past. Physical pain is the red flag trying to get your attention so that you can learn how to connect with the underlying emotions and release them.

How Emotional Vibrations Affect the Energy of our Organs

Having practised as a Naturopath, Kinesiologist and Energy Healer for over 23 years, I have created an emotional chart which offers an insight into how negative thoughts, emotions and feelings impact our physical body and our organs.

I can say with confidence and great pride that most, if not all, of the clients that have come to see me suffering with physical ailments have experienced a significant positive shift or change within their body after releasing emotional molecules, within days or even hours. Physical symptoms can simply disappear. This indicates that the underlying support network, the cellular system and organ function, experienced a rise in vitality and performance.

Returning to the negative thoughts and emotions, which become trapped or lodged in our organs, will in time attract the same destructive frequency back to them, creating a downward spiral.

The liver is the largest solid organ and the largest gland in the human body. It performs hundreds if not thousands of essential tasks. Classed as part of the digestive system, the main roles of the liver include detoxification, protein synthesis, and the production of chemicals that help digest the foods we eat.

Let us look at the signature vibration, anger. Anger vibrates at approximately 28 Hz and can manifest on different levels and areas of the mind-body system. Once this vibration gains density and amplitude, it will multiply within our system and attract more of the same frequency. This is the beginning of the downward spiral. If this is not recognised and dealt with in time, the vibration of anger will eventually attack every molecule, cell and organ within the entire mind-body system.

If the energy frequency of the liver becomes low, we may begin to experience a constant feeling of lethargy or fatigue and our joints may begin to become inflamed, causing discomfort and pain. If depleting frequencies multiply and start to dominate, the liver will be unable to function at a healthy level and in time will begin to present increasingly unhealthy symptoms.

Initially, the liver may present mild symptoms such as mood swings or imbalances within our endocrine system. However, once further depleted, it can lead to the development of skin conditions such as eczema or acne as well as various types of rash, causing itchiness and irritation. This is the result of our skin trying to flush out any excess toxins where the detoxifying organs are too depleted to do so. Our organs do not have the ability to verbally express which emotional vibrations are contributing to a functional imbalance; all it can do is present symptoms. It is only our level of self-awareness that will begin to create a link to our mind-body connection. Very often the trigger event lies somewhere in our past, usually having its roots set deep within one's childhood.

In my 23 years of experience as a practitioner, I would estimate that approximately 80 percent of my clients treated for inflammation in their joints present an overload of the signature vibration for anger. Anger, as well as other negative signature vibrational molecules, does not just accumulate in one organ alone. They have a tendency to spread throughout the entire mind-body system, affecting many of our vital organs.

Anger is one of the most depleting emotional vibrations and attacks everything within its path. It can contribute to hardening the walls of blood vessels and preventing absorption of nutrients and vitamins. It can harden the energy of the heart-centre, numb the intellect and suffocate the spirit within our most inner being. It can develop into a destructive fire-energy, which presents itself to me as the colour red when connecting to the energy body of my clients. Any inflammation creates cellular chaos. That in turn lowers our immune system and can very often end in serious ill health or other life threatening conditions.

I have created an emotional chart to give an approximate guide as to how the main depleting emotional frequencies are commonly presented, and which organs they most often affect on the energetic and physical level. This means that if negative emotional molecules are produced over a longer period of time they will inevitably deplete the energy level of the organ, followed by its physical depletion. Any negative or low vibration can stay hidden or suppressed anywhere within our mind-body system.

I believe that knowledge is empowering and the greater our understanding and the more enhanced awareness we have, the better we understand how our thoughts and emotions affect the entire mind-body system. Awareness is the most important step if we wish to evolve and self-heal. Stagnant emotional molecules need our attention and care. Anything negative that rises to the surface is a welcome opportunity for us to let it go and heal.

Chapter 5

Emotional Chart Guide

This is my personal chart based on my 23 years of experience treating clients.

Emotions that deplete liver energy:

- Anger
- Rage
- Resentment
- Vengefulness
- Irritability
- Unhappiness
- Bitterness
- Impatience

Emotions that deplete gallbladder energy:

- Resentment
- Rage
- Vengefulness
- Bitterness
- Anger
- Feeling helpless

- Hopelessness

Emotions that deplete spleen energy:

- Feeling rejected
- Anxiety
- Insecurity
- Envy
- Feeling isolated
- Over-analysing (negatively)
- Worry

Emotions that deplete stomach energy:

- Self-criticism
- Self-doubt
- Low self-esteem
- Self-judgement
- Disappointment
- Feeling deprived
- Nausea
- Greed
- Insecurity
- Worry

Emotions that deplete small intestine energy:

- Sorrow
- Sadness
- Nervousness

- Over-excitement
- Irritability
- Impatience
- Discouragement
- Internalisation
- Anger

Emotions that deplete large intestine energy:

- Guilt
- Grief
- Sorrow
- Regret
- Lack of self-worth
- Unworthiness
- Depression
- Sadness
- Apathy
- Disconnection
- Inability to let go

Emotions that deplete lung energy:

- Depression
- Sadness
- Fear
- Alienation
- Prejudice
- Unhappiness

- Trust issues

Emotions that deplete kidney energy:

- Fear
- Dread
- Panic
- Stress
- Phobias
- Irritability
- Anger
- Indecisiveness
- Superstition
- Insecurity

Emotions that deplete bladder energy:

- Anxiety
- Fear
- Terror
- Anger
- Fear of not being in control
- Trust issues
- Restlessness
- Frustration
- Hysteria
- Nervousness
- Worry
- Rigid thought system

Emotions that deplete heart energy:

- Hate
- Rage
- Anger
- Love (lack of)
- Envy
- Jealousy
- Resentment
- Bitterness
- Despair
- Grief
- Depression
- Self-love (lack of)

Chapter 6

Healing Symbols from a Higher Dimension for the Physical Body

During the period when I received the higher dimensional Healing Symbols, I channelled 11 healing symbols for the energy body and 11 healing symbols for the physical body. The vibrational imprint of the physical healing symbol is a slightly enhanced intensity, and targets specific energy layers within our anatomy.

The higher dimensional Healing Symbols help to dislodge stagnant energy clusters which were formed by depleting and low emotional vibrations. The higher dimensional Healing Symbols support the recalibration of the physical body by restoring cellular order.

The only language the body understands is the language of vibration. The quality of the vibration created by what we think and feel is heard and interpreted by our heart-brain-body system.

The vibration of the higher dimensional Healing Symbols for the physical body work on the following concept. The vibrational imprint is absorbed and transported to the anatomical sites.

In a similar way to how healing with sound works, the visual vibration of a healing symbol overrides the over-analytical mind and travels straight to the cell where it can transform and activate the healing process.

Your energy will instinctively be drawn towards the correct symbol for you in this moment. Those symbols you are not drawn to are not meant for your attention at this particular time. You may also be experiencing a subconscious resistance. Any of them may become the correct symbol for you at some point in the future.

Trust yourself to allow the correct symbol to surface and with a little practice you will begin to understand their messages and vibrations. You need to spend eight minutes gazing at your selected symbol, three times per day for 21 days. You can do this even if you have already chosen a healing symbol for healing your energy-emotional body.

If you have more than one ailment and are drawn to more than one symbol, you will need to decide which is your priority. You should not mix them randomly. You can use two Healing Symbols at the same time, but no more. In this case choose one symbol for one day and then use the other symbol the following day, alternating between the two symbols thereafter.

The Healing Symbol for the energy body is good to use alongside your chosen Healing Symbol for the physical body and will add to the healing process. Every moment you choose to spend connecting with your physical ailment, free of judgement, self-criticism and negative analytical mindset, is a step towards experiencing true healing.

You need to lovingly observe the emotions and feelings which have contributed to the depletion of your emotional and physical body, and then to explore the origins of the cause. Most importantly, allow yourself to connect with your feelings by engaging with the higher dimensional healing symbols.

As you gaze at the healing symbols, they may, after a period of time, appear to take on a slight motion and move gently around the page. This is good; simply continue your focus with a loving observation.

Before you begin, ensure that you are sitting comfortably and will not be disturbed or distracted. You will also need to adopt the rhythmic breathing technique explained below. Holding your breath or breathing incorrectly will weaken the healing effect of the symbol and is often caused by your subconscious resistance to letting go.

Breathing Technique

Take a deep breath in through your nose for four seconds, all the way down to your abdomen. Hold the breath for a further four seconds, then exhale slowly out through your slightly opened mouth for five seconds, allowing yourself to relax through the whole breath.

This technique should be repeated throughout the entire period that you are engaging with and observing each symbol. After each healing session, please drink a glass of purified water as this assists in flushing out negative emotional molecules.

Physical Body Healing Symbols

Symbol Name: Harmony

View this Healing Symbol from the top and follow the line all the way down to the bottom. Keep your gaze relaxed and your eye movement slow. Once at the bottom, return immediately to the top and repeat for eight minutes.

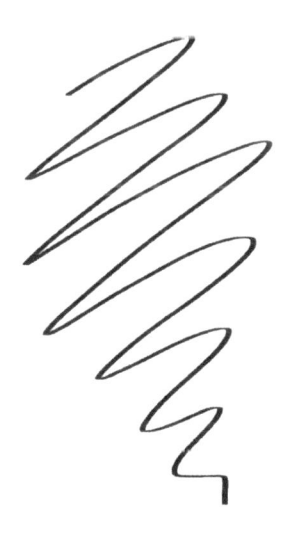

Healing Effects

- Extremely calming and soothing
- Balances the right brain hemisphere
- Stimulates the parasympathetic nervous system
- Calms the sympathetic nervous system
- Acts as a conductor and soothes the stressed brain

- Opens up the thoracic space
- Gives space to the heart and lungs
- Relaxes muscle tension in the upper back, especially the upper trapezius muscle in your neck-shoulder area
- Dislodges emotional vibrations of self-doubt and mental fatigue due to lack of trust in your own abilities
- Grounding

Symbol Name: Portal

View this Healing Symbol starting from the bottom left, working up to the top right. Keep your gaze relaxed and your eye movement slow. Once at the top, return immediately to the bottom and repeat for eight minutes.

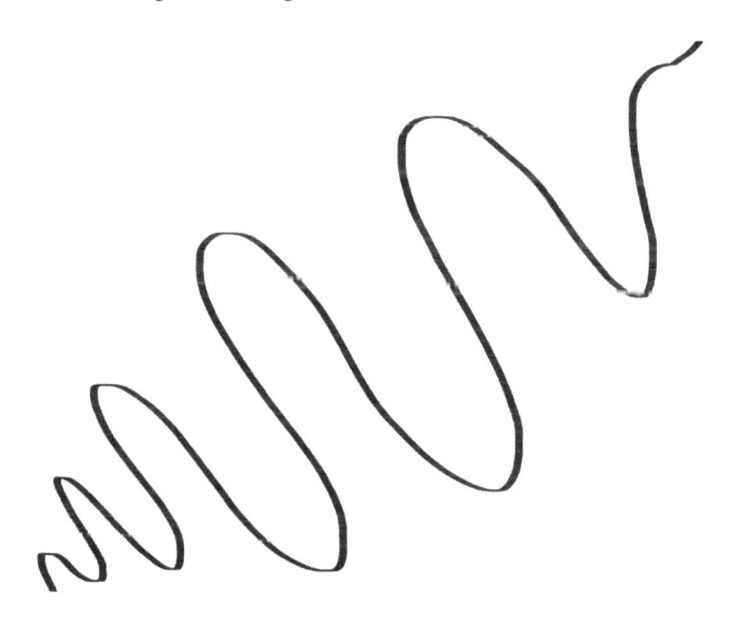

Healing Effects

- Activation of the creative energy from within
- Stimulates the right side of the brain and the pineal gland
- Helps with the release of stagnant energy in the left side of the body
- Helps to open up the energy of the spleen, pancreas,

stomach and small intestine
- Stimulates the release of oxytocin and serotonin (happy hormones)
- Creates a sense of uplift and joy

Helps to release the following emotional vibrations:

- Feeling rejected
- Pessimism
- Self-criticism
- Anxiety
- Low self-esteem
- Insecurity

Symbol Name: Peaceful Detachment

View this Healing Symbol starting at the bottom right corner, working up towards to the top left corner. Keep your gaze relaxed and your eye movement slow. Once at the top return immediately to the bottom and repeat for eight minutes.

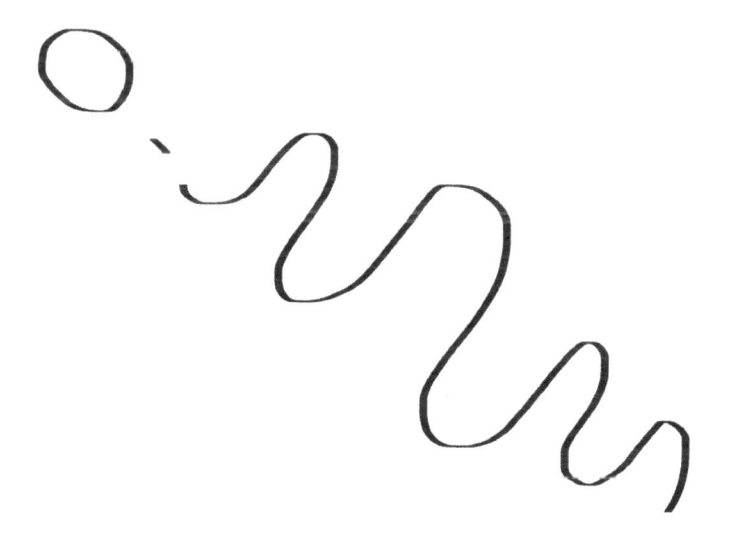

Healing Effects

- Relaxes the gallbladder
- Relaxes and decongests the liver
- Helps with letting go of the old and outworn patterns
- Detoxifying
- Supports the flow of the large intestine

Helps release the following emotional vibrations:

- Anger
- Frustration
- Irritation
- Guilt
- Self-judgement
- Impatience

Symbol Name: The Flow of Eight

View this Healing Symbol by beginning at the top right. Follow the loops to the left, down and back to the right in a figure of eight pattern all the way down to the end of the line. Keep your gaze relaxed and your eye movement slow. Once at the end, return immediately to the top and repeat for eight minutes.

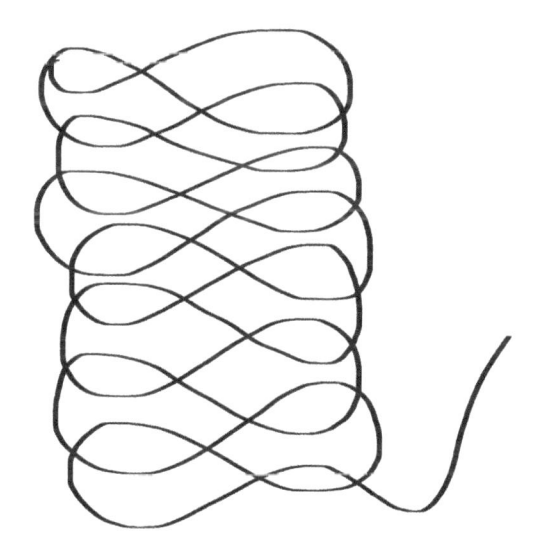

Healing Effects

- Calms the entire digestive system
- Stimulates the vagus nerve which helps to lower blood pressure
- Decreases heart rate
- Reduces the body's response to stress
- Helps with assimilation of information and allows it to be

digested at a healthy pace

Helps release the following emotional and physical vibrations:

- Disappointment
- Nausea
- Self-doubt
- Insecurity
- Low self-esteem
- Self-criticism

Symbol Name: Stabiliser

View this Healing Symbol starting at the top and follow through to the bottom. Keep your gaze relaxed and your eye movement slow. Once at the bottom, return immediately to the top and repeat for eight minutes.

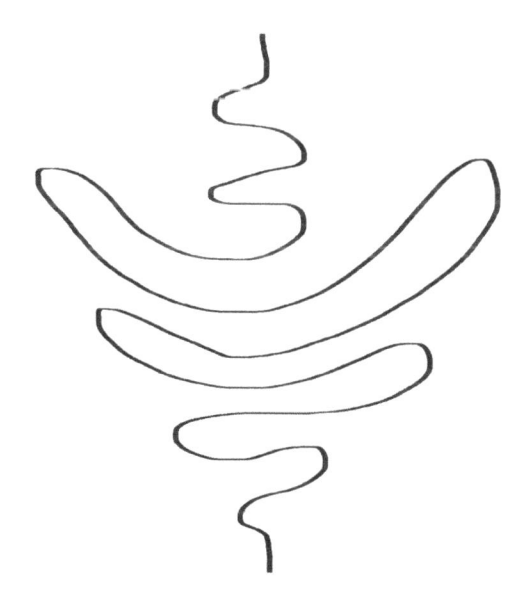

Healing Effects

- Strengthens the adrenal glands
- Soothes the adrenal glands

Helps release the following emotional vibrations:

- Anger
- Fear
- Anxiety

- Panic
- Terror
- Irritability
- Frustration

This Healing Symbol holds a particularly special vibrational imprint as it is very soothing and balancing for our adrenal glands. The adrenal glands, found above the kidneys, are endocrine glands that produce a variety of hormones including adrenaline, as well as the steroids aldosterone and cortisol, both of which help regulate metabolism, the immune system, blood pressure and our response to stress.

Continued levels of stress and anxiety drain the adrenal glands, suppress our immune system and leave us feeling constantly drained. In time, this can develop into a multitude of health issues, including burnout syndrome. It is therefore crucial that you focus on reducing stress in your adrenals at all times.

Symbol Name: Motion Flow

View this Healing Symbol starting from the left hand side of the top wave. Follow it across to the end on the right hand side. Go back to the left hand side and repeat for the second wave and then finally the third wave. Keep your gaze relaxed and your eye movement slow. Once you have completed the third wave, return immediately to the top wave and repeat for eight minutes.

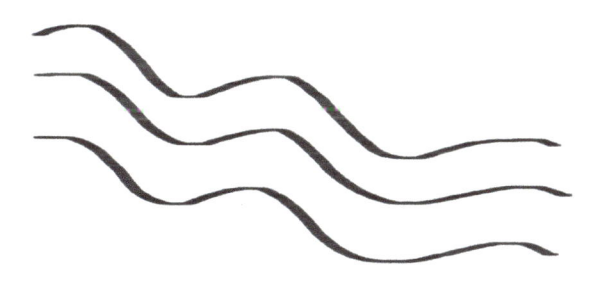

Healing Effects

This Healing Symbol stimulates the flow of our vascular system. It opens up the energy pathways which allow the cells to move more freely through our vessels. It helps smooth the inner lining of the mucus membranes and assists in supporting the healthy function of all the blood and lymphatic vessels of our circulatory and lymphatic systems.

It also stimulates the vagus nerve which holds a special place in our nervous system. The vagus nerve is the longest nerve of the autonomic nervous system and one of the most important nerves in the body. It helps to regulate many critical aspects of human physiology, including heart rate, blood pressure, sweating, digestion and even our speech.

Conditions such as diabetes or alcoholism can severely damage our nerves and also deplete the function of the vagus nerve. Anxiety, gastrointestinal diseases, and chronic inflammation (as a result of a low vibrational lifestyle and belief system) will in time suppress the vibration of the vagus nerve.

It is of the utmost importance to manifest balance for the body and mind, allowing ourselves to let go of any stress we have created or manifested within our mind-body system. Our body has an amazing ability to self-heal. We just need to allow it to do so.

Helps release the following emotional and physical vibrations:

- Stress
- Sluggishness
- Mental fatigue
- Physical fatigue
- Feeling stuck
- Fear
- Anger
- Resentment
- Inflammation

Symbol Name: Supple Flow

View this Healing Symbol starting at the top end of the left hand line. Follow it up, round and down to the bottom, then switch your gaze to the top of the right hand line and work down towards the bottom. The remainder of the eight minutes should be used to view this symbol as a whole, working up and down following the curvature while maintaining a relaxed gaze and a slow eye movement.

Healing Effects

This Healing Symbol helps to bring suppleness to a rigid spine and assists with decompression of the vertebrae. It helps to ease the energetic flow of the spine in the upper, middle and lower regions. The skeletal system should be regarded as our foundation or scaffold and plays a very important part in our vast energy mind-body system.

The quality of our thoughts and how we feel have an immediate impact on our skeletal system. For example, if we are feeling a lack of support, whether emotional or financial, we can develop compression and tension very quickly, especially if we resist exploring our underlying emotions and the quality of our lifestyle.

The structure and density of our bones can suffer greatly if we become rigid in our thinking. Examples can include not letting go of pride, an overactive ego and stubbornness. Our bones can also suffer if physical trauma has not been able to heal properly.

In addition, regular and prolonged poor posture whilst sitting or standing in fixed physical positions, such as those required in conjunction with the continuous use of computers and mobile phones, forces our musculo-skeletal system to maintain this unhealthy angle. Over time this can lead to the development of tension within the tissues of our muscles, which will contract and spasm, forcing the vertebrae out of alignment. The location of your back pain offers insight into the specific patterns which may have become trapped and need to be released.

Helps release the following emotional vibrations:

Upper Back

- Lack of emotional support
- Holding back love especially towards yourself
- Inability to forgive

Middle Back

- Feeling stuck in a situation
- Feeling trapped in a situation
- Inability to let go of the past
- False pride

Lower Back

- Feeling lonely
- Lack of financial support
- Fear of money
- Loss of confidence
- Instability
- Indecisiveness
- Insecurity

Symbol Name: Sacred Space

View this Healing Symbol starting at the top and follow the line into the centre. Keep your eyes gently fixated in the centre and allow yourself to become soft in body and to relax. Repeat for eight minutes.

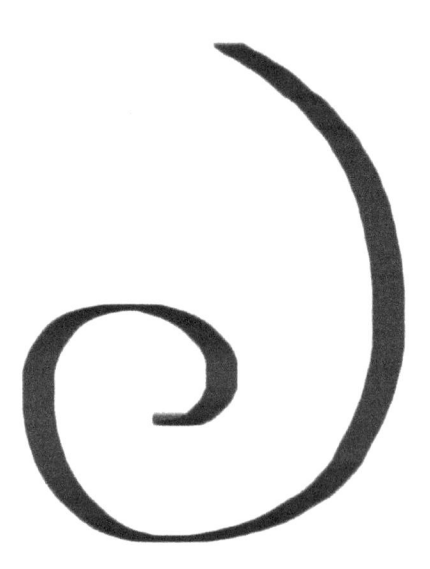

Healing Effects

This Healing Symbol is a space which invites you to relax, rest for a moment and take a deep breath. Allow yourself to make peace with what is. Surrender and accept yourself exactly as you are right now.

This Healing Symbol offers loving support and stability for the "wounded inner child" due to its nurturing vibrational imprint.

It is almost as if one is allowed to crawl back inside the womb of the "mother-earth-energy". It is a warm, gentle and loving safe space for your energy to relax and reflect.

Allowing yourself to pause in the pure moment of stillness can offer great healing energy. Thoughts ebb and flow, just like the waves of the ocean. There is no need to hold on to anything. Just sit and observe how you feel right now. Are you aware of feeling contracted or tight in any areas of your body? If so, bring your awareness to those areas and breathe into them until you feel less contracted. Look within using the eyes of unconditional love.

Helps release the following emotional vibrations:

- Low self-esteem
- Sense of loss
- Sorrow
- Grief
- Isolation
- Separation
- Loneliness
- Vulnerability

Symbol Name: Balance

View this Healing Symbol from top to bottom. Keep your gaze relaxed and your eye movement slow. Once at the bottom, return immediately to the top and repeat for eight minutes.

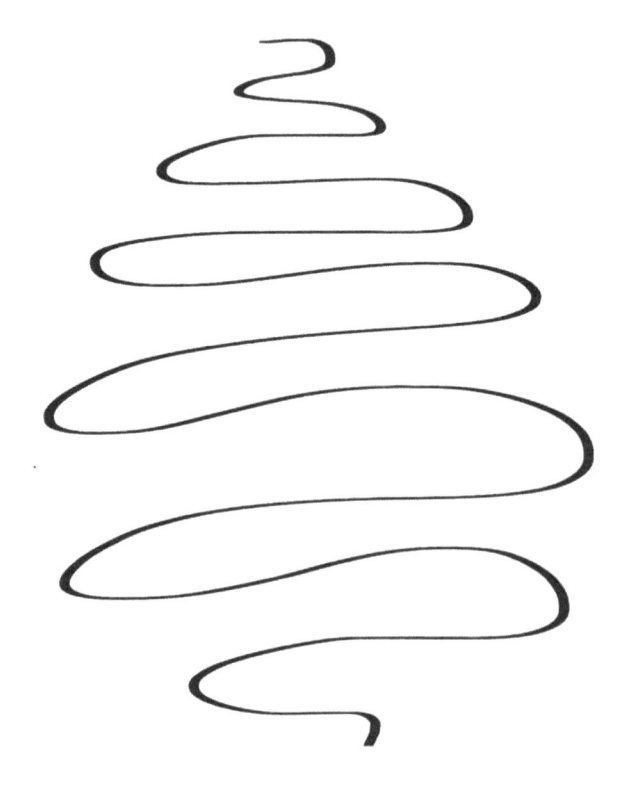

Healing Effects

This Healing Symbol helps with stabilisation and balancing of the brain at the times we lack focus or find ourselves being indecisive. If the hemispheres of our brain become imbalanced, we can begin to develop learning difficulties and conditions such as ADHD (Attention Deficit Hyperactivity Disorder).

In order to ensure that our brain can function and integrate both left and right brain hemispheres, it would be beneficial to perform physical, balance-based exercises in addition to eating a high vibrational diet.

Once the brain is balanced, our senses will become enhanced and be more open and able to absorb new information with ease.

There are many varieties of simple exercises that we can do to stimulate both brain hemispheres. During my development as a Kinesiologist, one of the many methods I learnt was the "Cross Crawl" method. This simple but very effective technique benefits all age groups and is performed as follows:

Standing comfortably, slowly begin by slapping your right hand onto the sole of your left foot, then your left hand onto your right foot. Do this first in front of you and then repeat the procedure but slapping the soles of your feet behind you, crossing from left to right as you go. Try to create a flow in motion as if you are dancing.

If you are unable to bend, you can also do this exercise seated by slapping your knees, using the same routine, instead of your feet. It only takes a few minutes and is great to use when taking a short break away from the computer or work desk.

Helps release the following emotional vibrations:

- Indecisiveness
- Mood swings

- Lack of focus
- Irritability
- Nervousness
- Restlessness
- Insecurity
- Inflexibility

In addition, this Healing Symbol supports the stabilisation of the atlas and axis vertebrae, the two most superior bones in the vertebral column. Together they support and join the skull to the other five cervical vertebrae, allowing the normal movement of our head. The atlas is the topmost bone that sits just below the skull. When we become stressed and suffer with negative emotional vibrations as described above, the atlas can become lodged onto the axis vertebra, which will create compression down the entire spine.

It also helps with the improvement of the inner ear function, which assists with stability when walking. Sometimes the inner ear hairs can become rigid and will lose their efficiency to vibrate. When this happens, we lose stability and balance making the most natural of motions such as walking extremely difficult, as well as causing dizziness and symptoms of vertigo.

Symbol Name: Cleanser

View this Healing Symbol starting from the centre and follow the line anti-clockwise until you reach the very bottom. Keep your gaze relaxed and your eye movement slow. Once at the bottom, return immediately to the centre and repeat for eight minutes.

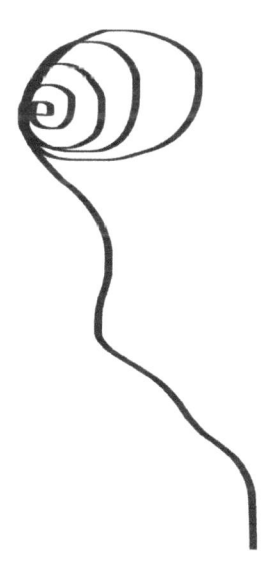

Healing Effects

This symbol offers healing for the upper cranium, the eyes and the sinuses. It also helps to detoxify and dislodge stagnant energy from the third eye and solar plexus energy centres.

It improves the flow of lymphatic fluid in the lymphatic system, which is responsible for the removal of waste material from the cells and tissues.

The symbol Cleanser will help the absorption and distribution of fats from the digestive system. It supports the movement of white blood cells (part of the immune system) to and from the lymph nodes and from the bone marrow where they are made. Cleanser is great for indigestion created by emotional overload. It also assists in soothing inflammation in our nervous system.

The third eye is located centrally between our eyebrows and is connected to the pineal gland, which is located in the centre of our brain. The solar plexus energy centre is located just below the sternum in the stomach area, which is also a central point for many organs such as the stomach, spleen, pancreas, gallbladder, liver and small intestine.

On an emotional level, it resonates with aspects of self-worth and how we value ourselves. Sometimes we can hold a lot of resentment towards ourselves. For example, if we are unable to forgive ourselves for making what we perceive to have been wrong decisions in the past, or for making the same mistakes over and over again. Disliking ourselves or feeling that we are unlovable as we are is a hotbed for triggering a multitude of depleting vibrational molecules.

Helps release the following emotional and physical vibrations:

- Anger
- Unworthiness
- Guilt
- Shame
- Resentment
- Inflammation

Symbol Name: Peaceful Heart

View this Healing Symbol starting in the top centre and follow it all the way down to the bottom centre. Keep your gaze there for a moment and then return to the top centre. Repeat for eight minutes.

Healing Effects

Peaceful Heart, as the name suggests, helps to soothe and calm the heart centre and assists in reconnecting with your inner being or higher self. This symbol attracts the highest vibration of love and forgiveness into our heart centre.

Any pain we endure in our past wants to heal, but the healing process only reaches its climax at the moment of acceptance and forgiveness. Many of us walk through life clinging onto the past through unexpressed emotions and the resistance to forgiveness.

Helps release the following emotional vibrations:

- Broken heart
- Bitterness
- Separation anxiety
- Lack of self-love
- Lack of intuition
- Feeling disconnected
- Sorrow
- Sense of abandonment

Why Do we Struggle to Forgive?

Releasing old attachments would propel us into the unknown and generate feelings of fear. We feel that we need to cling on to the negativity because it is the only thing we know and have accepted it as our truth. We are under the false belief that if we forgive, then the perpetrator will be released and forgiven for what they have done to us.

In order to free ourselves from the painful chains of the past, we need to surrender and forgive. We need to forgive every aspect of the event including the perpetrator and ourselves. Once we practice forgiveness, the higher vibration of love and inner peace replaces the old and outworn negative past, allowing our mind-body system to heal. Holding onto past pain, especially trapped within the heart centre, can contribute towards disease of the heart (heartbreak) and harden the walls of the arteries and our blood vessels.

Practicing regular meditation, in particular heart meditation, is very healing. I have created one for those of you requiring some heart healing. You can find this on YouTube under 'Britta Hochkeppel Heart Meditation'.

Chapter 7

Awareness

Becoming Aware

We wake up every morning thinking the same thoughts and focusing on the same problems. We get out the same side of the bed and follow our daily routines. We follow the same rituals every day, whether they are bathroom or breakfast rituals, or simply getting ready for work. Then we drive the same way to work. We see and speak to the same colleagues. This becomes our routine, our program, which means it is stored in our body too.

By the age of 35, 95% of what we think we are is only a memorised set of behaviours and emotional reactions. Our attitudes, beliefs and perceptions function like a computer program whereby we begin to run on auto-pilot. We only like to look at what is familiar to us, resisting any change, but it prevents us from evolving.

How we think and feel creates our state of being. A familiar past becomes our predictable future. On an emotional level, we are quite lazy and often wait for external changes to occur which eventually force us into making changes. Unfortunately, these changes are often accompanied by pain, illness or loss, as we have simply ignored all the previous signs of our emotional, mental or physical body's attempt to grab our attention.

We spend so much time and focus on aspects experienced years ago that we prevent ourselves from being in the present moment. We often fail to realise that it is we who create the resistance to letting go, to moving forward and evolving, or raising our vibrational state.

We spend so much time explaining to others why we are unhappy or in pain. We are masters of creating excuses. For example, we may say something like, 'Once I earn more money, I can begin to focus on a course that I have always wanted to do', or 'Once life gets easier, I can change my habits and behaviours'. Instead, we need to become more aware.

First of all, we need to realise that we are vibrational beings who emit and transmit frequencies all day and all night. These frequencies are created by our thoughts, emotions and generated feelings. It is our individual vibrational imprint that we send out into the Universe, or the Quantum Field, which is mirrored back to us. We experience the mirror of our vibration.

Then there is another part in us which is known as our inner being, or our higher self. It is our source energy, what we were before we were born into our physical body and this life. It is our inner being or higher self which is home to our source of awareness. I believe that it is our saviour. All we need to do is afford ourselves the time to reconnect to it. Our inner being is free from any presence of ego or our negatively conditioned belief system.

With awareness we have the ability to blend into that non-physical existence and become the vibrational frequency of each and every new request that we have sent forth from our own physical experiences.

Our vibrational reality is our true reality. As we travel through our life's experiences, our inner being stands beside us and absorbs the fullness of who we have become up until this moment. Based on the conclusions we have drawn from our past experiences, we decide what is good for us and what isn't, and ask for improvements.

We have become so skilled at wasting time and energy in expressing to others in detail what and where our life lacks and why, that we are unable to do what we were born to do. We are blissfully unaware that it is the vibration of our thoughts and generated feelings that creates our current signature vibration. We broadcast this signature vibration that is very much received by the surrounding energy field, the Quantum Field, that matches and mirrors it back to us on a vibrational level.

This exterior field that we perceive to be invisible consists of energy and matter, with a very similar appearance and interaction to how cells are arranged and function in our own brain. This parallel relationship between our brain and the Universe facilitates a two way dialogue that explains how we can manifest thoughts into reality.

We are in a continuous dialogue with the Universe, as indeed it is with us. Many scientists are recognising that what we are experiencing on planet Earth is a mirror of our collective psychic waste and our negative thoughts. These are created by limiting beliefs and low vibrational thoughts and feelings about ourselves and others, reinforced by the devastation we witness that is created by our mass constant global off-loaded negative vibrations.

Greed, violence, selfishness and ignorance are just some of the negative low vibrations we emit. Dumped vibrational waste is still energy, and negative energy accumulates in any area where there is more of the same; similar to our emotional vibrations getting trapped in specific anatomical sites inside our body.

We need to become aware and understand that every single

human being currently living on this planet is influencing the entire planet with the quality of their thoughts, emotions and generated feelings. We are not a separate form: we are all energetically linked to each other and everything that ever was and is. We need to wake up to the fact that our collective desire to improve our life quality by raising our vibration will result not only in raising our own vibration but, more importantly, in raising the electromagnetic vibration of planet Earth, benefiting all animals and nature.

We, as a global family, need to realise that we are all influencers. We decide which level of suffering and pain we wish to continue to manifest, or we can choose to vibrate with a higher frequency and contribute towards manifesting abundance and unconditional love with the time given to us on this planet.

Chapter 8

Your Belief System is Your Healer

It is not the Healer placing his or her hands on your head who is bringing about the healing. It is your belief that has the power to heal you. Your belief system can heal you, but it can also make you very sick.

Healing is self-healing. We now know that our mind is not static and our thoughts create energy, and that the quality of our thoughts change neural networks. Good thoughts make beneficial neural pathways and bad thoughts facilitate disadvantageous neural pathways.

The mind is extremely gifted at talking to the body. However, it is unable to distinguish between the vibration of a bad memory, created by experiencing an actual physical trauma, or the same chemical response, created by practicing a negative inner dialogue.

A negative conversation with your mind results in a negative response. If we think negative thoughts, like for example, 'I ate that piece of cake and now I am going to get fat', then we tend to look for the validation, not realising that it is our negative belief and focused negative thought commanding our brain to release the necessary chemicals to initiate the weight gain. Then the next day we receive the physical validation that we have gained some weight. Our ego will recognise this as confirmation and we will say, 'I knew it, I only have to look at a piece of cake and it makes me gain weight'.

Our commands are so powerful that our brain reacts accordingly by releasing more stress hormones, such as cortisol, which will enhance our appetite for foods higher in sugar, from which we will gain weight.

In the same way, people who believe that they can eat what they want often stay the same weight and size even though they consume larger portions of food or eat more frequently. However, I am not suggesting you should go and eat unhealthy low vibrational foods in excess!

Your mind communicates with your body constantly, and now, since you understand the power of vibrations created by thought alone, it is your responsibility to be mindful, aware and have a positive conversation with your mind.

'I am a perfect weight.'

'I am of perfect health.'

'Everything I do is perfect for me.'

Remember, your words shape your reality, so only change your words if you wish to change your reality. We are all guilty of practising a negative inner dialogue from time to time. Most of us are unaware, up to now, that thoughts and emotions have their own signature vibrations which command our mind to react, and the brain to manifest what we have asked for.

Tell your mind you feel amazing. Your mind will accept and manifest anything you command. It is the vibration that your body understands.

The Rules of the Mind

I have been practising Naturopathy, Kinesiology and Energy Healing for over 23 years, and I am a great believer that you cannot fix what you do not understand or lack awareness in. You cannot heal what you cannot feel, and in order to feel, you must be aware.

So, I would like to take you through some of the typical mind traps which create mind blocks and keep us stuck in the same thought patterns. Read the following lines one at a time. After each one, close your eyes and try to get an impression of how it makes you feel.

'I am going to try and remember what the rules of the mind are.'

'It is so hard to memorise this stuff.'

'If only I could memorise something.'

'I wish I had a better memory.'

'I hope I can remember the rules of the mind.'

Adopting this type of negative language with your mind will give you a sense of your energy dropping. This drop is caused by the reaction of your mind-body to receiving these depleting vibrations.

So, to start any of your sentences with, 'I wish', 'I hope' or 'I'll try', is not confirming a positive command and therefore you cannot expect to manifest any positive changes relating to the rest of the sentence.

We would not say, 'I wish I could pick up that pen to write something' or 'I wish I could pick up my toothbrush to clean my teeth', we simply do it.

By beginning our internal mind dialogue with, 'I wish' or 'I try', your mind will respond with a resignation reaction and your brain will respond with something similar to, 'Yes, I wish you could do it too. Let's just forget it.'

If instead, you choose to say to yourself, 'I have a phenomenal memory, my memory is awesome, I love to learn new things, I remember everything', you are creating a command which your brain will see as a rule and create a 3D image to confirm it.

Your words have an immense power and you must learn with new-found awareness to choose positive words, feeding your mind with new higher vibrational commands. If thoughts and words have this amount of power and you get to choose what you say, then expect amazing things. Recognise that power and manifest the best for yourself.

Chapter 9

How to Raise your Vibration

Meditate Daily

You may have noticed that meditation is gaining massive popularity. Backed by thousands of scientific studies, prescribed by doctors and practised by many of the world's wisest people, the reasons why you should incorporate meditation into your daily life are overwhelming.

According to Dr. Bruce Lipton, a prominent author and highly respected cell researcher, stress is the cause of at least 95% of all disease. If there is an all-natural, super effective solution to fundamentally transform how your body responds to this so-called "silent killer", then here it is – meditation.

As mentioned previously, negative emotions and depleting belief systems lower our vibrational state immensely. The seemingly endless supply of stress and negativity in modern life causes us to experience dysfunctional emotions such as anger, resentment, fear, shame, guilt and sadness, which pile up year after year, layer upon layer.

All of this can take a major toll on your health and create a downward spiral of worsening symptoms. Meditation is the best way to increase your vibrational frequency. It can cancel out unhealthy brainwave patterns, cool off our overheated sympathetic nervous system, strengthen our weaker brain regions and flood us with happy hormones.

Meditation only requires between 10 and 25 minutes of your time, once or twice a day. There are many different meditation techniques:

- Mindful meditation
- Spiritual meditation
- Focused meditation
- Movement meditation
- Mantra meditation
- Transcendental meditation

To find the meditation technique that suits you best, you need to explore them and tune into which one leaves you feeling the most relaxed or "aware".

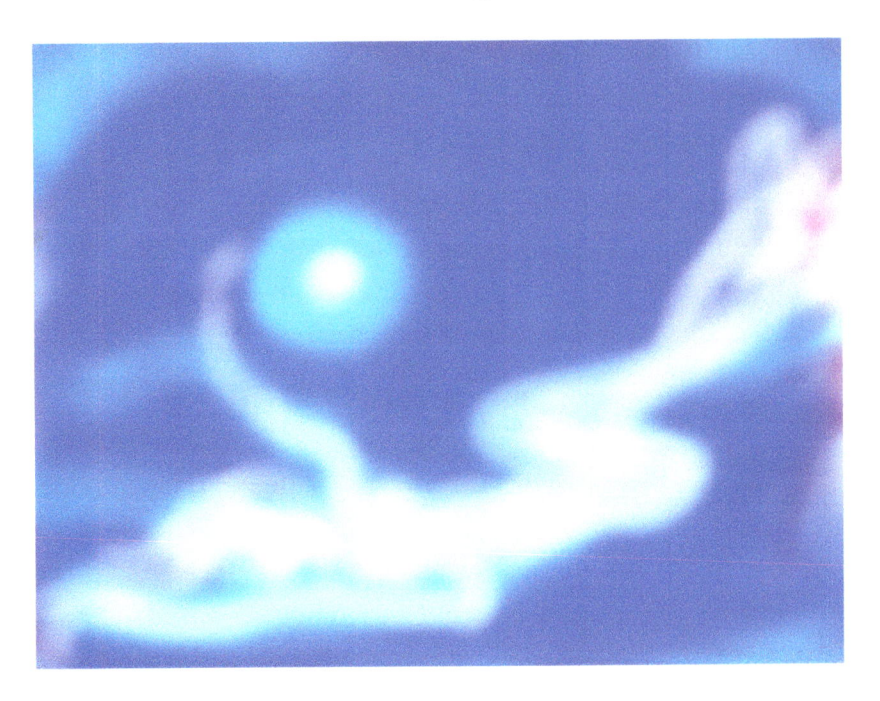

Mindful Meditation

During mindful meditation, you pay attention to your thoughts as they pass through your mind. You do not judge them or become involved in them; you simply just observe them. This practice combines concentration with awareness.

You may find it helpful to observe your breath or bodily sensations during your meditation. This technique is good for people who enjoy practising alone and who do not have a teacher.

Spiritual Meditation

Spiritual meditation is used in Eastern religions, such as

Hinduism and Daoism. It is similar to prayer in that you reflect in the silence around you and seek a deeper connection with your God or Universe.

Essential oils are commonly used to heighten this experience. Popular oils include: frankincense, sage, myrrh, sandalwood, palo santo, and cedar. This meditation can be practised in a place of worship or at home.

Focused Meditation

This technique involves concentration using any of the five senses.

You can focus on something internal, i.e. your breath, or counting Malta beads, or listening to a gong. This requires you to be able to hold your focus and may be difficult for beginners.

Movement Meditation

This practice may include simple exercise or activities such as walking through the woods, gardening, jogging or riding a bicycle, or alternatively for the more advanced, Qi Gong or Tai Chi. It is an active form of meditation where the movement guides you and is particularly popular amongst the left brain dominant male energy.

Mantra Meditation

This type of meditation uses a repetitive sound to clear the mind. It can be a word or phrase, such as the popular "Om".

Here it is not important if the mantra used is spoken quietly or loudly. Tune into what feels right for you.

Transcendental Meditation

Transcendental meditation is the most popular type of meditation around the world and it's the most scientifically studied. This practise is more customisable than mantra meditation, using a mantra or series of words that are specific to each practitioner. It is a great technique for those who love structure.

Mindful Breathing Method

You can practise this breathing technique almost anywhere, but it would be ideal if you can find a quiet place to do it. Sit down and close your eyes, resting your hands in your lap. Bring your awareness to the touch of your body on your seat. Feel the weight of your body on your chair or cushion.

Find a comfortable posture.

Following a positive mind mantra is also very helpful, so let us use the following: 'Let go and breathe in the goodness that you are.' Inhale deeply through your nose all the way down into your abdomen and hold your breath for five to six seconds. Exhale through your slightly opened mouth, making a soft 'haaaa' sound for about six seconds.

Be mindful that when you exhale using the 'haaaa' sound you let go of any tension, stress, anxiety, anger or any other negatively charged emotional vibrations. As you inhale, imagine that you are breathing in healing and purifying energy. Repeat eight times.

In my personal experience, I find that repeating it eight times helps to connect deeper with the energy field surrounding us. When you feel ready to try out or add other techniques, there are plenty to choose from.

Another mindful technique that works for me is to sit practising a deep breathing method while using high frequency words such as 'gratitude', 'peace' or 'unconditional love'.

As you breathe in, imagine the vibration of gratitude pouring into every cell of your body and inner being. As you exhale, let go of any negative emotions that surface. Never judge or analyse anything which comes to the surface, but instead be grateful that it is emerging into your awareness to be released.

You can repeat the mindful breathing methods once or twice a day. Particularly, last thing before you sleep can be very helpful.

Raise your Vibration with Crystals

Crystals are a creation of nature and have been used for centuries, not only for their beauty but also for healing due to their intense energetic properties.

We know that everything is energy and that everything is influenced by its interaction with other fields. The crystal energy field interacts with the energy field of humans whereby information is transmitted between the crystal and the human via the resonant frequencies occurring in each field.

A crystal with the correct or matching energy frequency properties can resonate with a particular condition in the human with great healing results.

Before connecting and choosing your supporting crystal to help you raise your vibration, I would recommend a visit to a crystal shop where you can explore the crystals, using your sense of touch to feel combined with your eyes to see which are the right crystals for you. The one that is right for your energy will draw you in. Something will stand out and speak to you or connect with your inner being. Allow yourself to explore and be guided by the crystal: there is no need to rush into it.

When you have chosen your crystal or crystals, look into the healing properties it offers. You may be surprised to recognise the accuracy and detail within the description and how much it resonates with your current situation, and where you require support or healing.

I have worked with crystals for over 25 years. When in recovery from major operations or experiencing other life lessons, I have learnt to value the variety of amazing vibrations gifted to us by Mother Nature.

Crystals transmit their signature vibration into the surrounding energy field and can also be used to enhance the vibration within rooms and buildings. All crystals raise your vibration and each one has its own unique signature vibrational qualities. Inform yourself how to clean your crystal and where it is best kept if not in use. For the greatest healing effect, wear your chosen crystal on your skin.

Become a Positive Thinker

Be at peace with what is, no matter what it is. To be at peace with oneself is a beautiful place to be, and one which has a high frequency. Most of us spend far too much time in our headspace, focusing on our negative past experiences. We can spend a lot of time dwelling on who has done us wrong, or who has hurt us the most.

We need to learn to waste less time thinking negatively about our past and more time focusing on the positive experiences presented to us. This focus can bring a heightened awareness, leading you to become a better version of yourself. If you continue a daily routine of dwelling on the negative aspects of your past, your energy frequency will be lowered, leading to an array of ailments and illness as a result of a suppressed immune system.

A new life starts with changes in your way of thinking. Self-judgement needs to become a thing of the past. Communicate with your inner being in a calm and soothing tone and be proud of all your achievements, including the mistakes. By injecting positive energy and enthusiasm into the quality of your inner dialogue, the relationship with yourself will improve, leading to a greater sense of wellbeing.

Try to look for the positive in everything that you come into contact with, and view everything from the most positive perspective. Positive inner dialogue raises your vibration. Let go and trust the flow of life.

All too often we end up self-sabotaging our lives by trying to control every event within it. Wanting everything now, or for things to happen in the way we believe that they should, can create a high level of resistance to the flow of life. This resistance will lead to us missing out on opportunities that we fail to see because we are too busy trying to manipulate the course of events.

The personality trait of being too controlling is born out of fear. It arises as a defence mechanism in an attempt to protect ourselves from repeating traumatic emotional experiences that have been suffered in the past.

Fear is one of the most depleting emotional vibrations and suffocates any positivity or creativity. It transforms every moment into doubt and can give rise to insecurities that, in time, can become overwhelming unless the underlying fear is properly addressed.

Once we allow ourselves to face our fears and lovingly harness them, we can begin to say yes to life and stop standing in our own way. Pay attention to any negative emotions, thoughts or beliefs you hold in connection with yourself and then decide whether you feel you deserve to be happy and successful.

Give yourself permission to be happy and successful, no matter what you have thought or felt in the past; whether that be from childhood, a year ago or a moment ago. We are in constant motion and with every new moment we have the opportunity to manifest a new and better version of ourselves.

Self–Love

How does it make you feel when I ask, 'Do you love yourself?' Do you get a sense of contraction within your heart centre or solar plexus centre, or do you feel a warmth and light from within?

Most of us travel through life burdened by multiple layers of negative beliefs. We have often duplicated them from our parents, or created a distorted truth as a result of our observations since childhood. Subconsciously, we have accepted negative, self-limiting beliefs because we have decided that they are true.

We all have the potential to be the most advanced intellectual beings with high status on a personal level. However, too often our mind is listening to the distorted voice of our scarred inner child. In reality, this is the only thing that prevents us from fulfilling our true potential.

If you begin to think positively about yourself and love yourself, your emotional frequency will elevate to a higher level. As a result, you will be able to love and be loved unconditionally.

Never look back with feelings of shame, guilt or blame. Some of your life experiences will have been more important than others. However, each of those experiences will have enabled you to learn something new about yourself whilst you were continuing to evolve.

Ask yourself: 'What have I learnt from my experiences? How has this experience helped me evolve into an even better version of myself?'

Manifesting your Desires into Reality

Your thoughts and feelings must be in harmony with each other. Think of what you desire and create the feeling as if it is already part of your reality. Once your thoughts and feelings are in vibrational harmony, the Universe will mirror them, manifesting them into reality.

To give you an example; many years ago, I was running a ladies' boutique alongside my healing practice. I wanted to let that part of my life go, as it had never held a place in my heart. However, 2013 was not the best time to sell a business and I'd been advised by many that I probably wouldn't be able to sell it for anywhere near its worth.

As a strong believer in the law of attraction, I decided to use a visualisation technique in order to help me to sell my business.

I visualised finding a female buyer within eight weeks who would buy all my existing stock whilst keeping my staff employed, so they too would continue earning money doing what they enjoy.

I visualised myself shaking hands on the deal whilst creating the feeling of happiness for everyone involved. I felt so light and relieved that I had been able to sell all my stock and ensure the happiness of my staff. I even imagined them laughing with each other and the new owner. I repeated this twice a day for a few weeks whilst ignoring the negative influences around me.

To the surprise of everyone, eight weeks later I sold the business just as I had visualised. My thoughts and feelings had been mirrored by the Universe, confirmed by sending the female buyer to me, and manifested exactly as I had created it in my mind. Everyone was happy, especially me, for now I was able to focus on doing what I was born to do.

This technique can work for you, too. Whatever it is you desire, be clear about what you want. Visualise and feel it, as if it has already happened and is part of your reality. You need to be consistent and persistent, and understand that it is the vibration of your thoughts combined with your generated feelings that lead to them manifesting into reality.

How to Think High Frequency Thoughts

Observe your Thoughts

The first thing to do is to begin to become conscious of your thoughts. Too often negative thoughts sneak in through the back door of your mind and make you feel worse. Negative thoughts have a bad habit of attracting more of the same and produce new negative experiences, which you may say is bad luck or coincidence. It is the result of a negative thought which has emanated and attracted the mirror of the low vibration back into our energy field.

Suffocate Negative Thoughts immediately

Treat negative thoughts like an unwanted intruder or a naughty child. If you become aware of one, make yourself stop thinking it immediately. Nullify the negative by making yourself think about something beautiful or empowering, or connect with a clear happy memory.

Create an image of your vision - a beautiful landscape or object - and in time you will have positive images available in a fraction of a second. You need to stay consistent and allow your brain to learn new techniques. Be patient in your progress.

Be the Solution

The moment you are facing a problem, see the solution or ask yourself: 'What would it take for me to find a solution in this situation? What am I learning here?' Understand that problems do not exist, only lessons. Sometimes what we consider to be hurtful or see as a problem that we have to deal with can often be a blessing in disguise.

For example, we might yearn to be in a loving relationship but cannot seem to find a suitable partner. We can feel lonely and sometimes abandoned, or we can question if we are loveable as we are. Sometimes we need more time to learn to love ourselves first before we can attract what we desire into our life.

Everything that happens is happening *for* you, not against you. It is only your negative belief system and thoughts that lower your vibration if you allow them to.

Get your Blood Pumping

Thoughts and emotions generate vibration. Vibration requires movement, and the more we move the better we feel. Physical exercise is much more than just maintaining shape and fitness; it also allows emotional vibrations to move about and to be released.

Physical exercise is especially beneficial for people who are mentally depleted or suffering with anxiety, depression and other mental imbalances. So, become active! Walk, cycle, dance or do whatever you enjoy. The more you move, the happier you will feel and the more you will draw happy experiences into your energy.

Believe in Yourself

A strong belief in yourself and your projects increases your frequency, its outcome and the level of success. Positives, such as success or feeling happy with where you are in your journey and career, have a high frequency. The stronger you believe in something, the quicker it can manifest for you.

Raise your Lifestyle

Raising your lifestyle or quality of life starts with being aware of the many beautiful moments which are gifted to you each and every day.

- Enjoying the aroma of your morning coffee or listening to the birdsong of the blackbird at dawn.
- Creating a loving and personal living space that makes you feel safe and cosy.
- Treating yourself to your favourite flowers or choosing nice clothes to wear.
- Buying your favourite foods and cooking yourself one of your favourite meals.
- Snuggling up with your pet on the sofa and enjoying the tranquil moments of unwinding and sitting in each other's energy.
- Reading your favourite book or dancing to your favourite tune.

Whatever you improve about your lifestyle or home will make you feel better and raise your vibrational state.

Practicing Kindness

We all know how good it feels to be of service or to help others. Giving to someone else (without expecting anything in return) raises your vibration from, 'I don't have enough' to 'I have more than enough to give'. This generates the vibration of abundance and this high vibration will create more of the same.

Here are some examples of how you can raise your vibration by practicing kindness.

- Involve a person into a friendly conversation and make them feel less separate and lonely.
- Notice something nice about someone and let them know.
- Help to carry an elderly person's shopping back to their home or help them across the street.
- Call a friend who you haven't seen or spoken to for a while to ask how they are.
- Offer your services free of charge. For example, undertake voluntary work.

Keep Learning

Learning and living with an open and inquisitive mind also raises your frequency. Learning something new allows you to grow and to feel good about yourself. Knowledge is a great soother of fear, for we often fear the unknown. Learning something new which we may have feared in our past immediately equips us with new solutions to improve our life quality.

If you have not learnt something new in a while, why not explore, for example, learning how to play an instrument, or a new language, or how to paint. The brain loves to learn new things and that raises our vibrational state.

Smile and Laugh Often

Put a smile on your face! Whenever you are feeling sad or low, smile. Your inner being will register the expression and release happy hormones. Even if you have to force it a little, with time you will feel better.

Allow yourself to laugh whenever possible. Today's world can be a very serious place and we don't laugh enough. Laughing releases a whole chain of vitality-enhancing chemicals into our body system. Why not watch your favourite comedy or a funny movie? Put an image with a smiling face onto the bathroom mirror! Surround yourself with positive people.

It is really important to give yourself permission to be happy and to laugh, despite the suffering around you. Allowing your energy to become low or drained will not ease their suffering. On the contrary, on a vibrational level you help by keeping your vibrational state high, as explained in previous chapters. The higher you raise your vibration, the higher the amount of positive energy particles you will emanate into your surroundings.

Eat High Vibrational Foods

Different foods vibrate at different frequencies; some high and some low. For example, broccoli has a high vibration as do blueberries, whereas biscuits, crisps and 'fast food' do not vibrate at all. When choosing your foods, take them as nature offers. Stay away from or drastically reduce the consumption of processed and packaged foods. If you are consuming processed foods that have chemicals and pesticides added to them, or foods which are packaged in plastic, these will significantly lower your vibration.

Conversely, consuming good quality organic produce as nature intended will generate a high vibration and support your entire mind-body system. Eating wholesome foods will help to raise your frequency within your organs. This in turn helps you maintain physical strength and high immunity, supporting your defence system against pollution and toxins that we come into daily contact with.

Pay attention to how eating certain foods make you feel. If you feel sluggish or tired, heavy or phlegmy after eating certain foods, you will benefit from eating less of them or removing them from your diet in favour of a more wholesome food choice.

Everything is vibration and the food we eat emanates vibrational particles into our digestive system. Whilst we eat, we absorb the energetic imprint of the foods as well as the minerals and vitamins. A healthy gut supports a healthy mind and a happy mind generates happy thoughts.

Drink Water

Always ensure that you drink plenty of water. Purified or filtered water is best. Drinking good quality water daily is essential for us to flush out the toxins within our system. I use a reverse osmosis water filtration system which filters out fluoride, bacteria, viruses, pesticides, chemicals and more.

Drinking low vibrational water will drain your body and overwhelm your system. Low quality water enhances calcification of the pineal gland which, once damaged, is difficult to repair. Investing in a good quality water filtration system is an investment in your health.

We produce toxins with every passing moment that is our own biological cellular waste. This waste is produced by our organs, our thoughts and our emotional vibrations. We absolutely need water to help us flush out all the various toxins, including old and outworn thought patterns.

The Magical Vibration of Gratitude

One of the highest vibrations and one that is very precious to me is the signature vibration of gratitude. Expressing gratitude to others, ourselves and our lives induces positive emotions, primarily happiness.

Gratitude can boost the neurotransmitter serotonin and activate the brain to produce dopamine. When you feel grateful, you experience synchronised activation of many parts within your brain, giving you positive effects all over. It is scientifically proven that living in a state of gratitude balances the entire mind-body system.

Gratitude can:

- improve self-esteem
- increase mental strength
- enhance physical strength
- allow more of the same to enter your energy

Once we learn to say 'thank you' for anything and everything that we encounter in our daily lives, we will soon begin to notice that everything around us starts to change. Saying thank you is almost like a "magic word" which acts as a magnet to allow all the high vibrational things to enter our lives. One has to stay consistent and stay in this mindset for several days, free of judgement and doubt. Try it and see what you experience.

Chapter 10

Living in a Higher Vibrational State

A person who lives in a state of high vibration and unity with the Quantum Field will initially not appear different from others. It is when you begin to stand in their energy or hear them speak that you can sense a light emanating from them.

People who are connected have an inner knowing, a deep sense of trust that the Universe has their back and that everything is exactly as it should be. They are not influenced or seduced by others who are still living in a vibrational state of resistance. They know that the Universe has an invisible force and an infinite supply to all that wish to partake in it.

The person who is connected lives in a constant state of gratitude. They are thankful for everything, even things that might be seen as an obstacle. They own the ability to understand the underlying message or lesson of their illness or situation, allowing them to move on. Rather than asking 'why me?' they surrender into the process with heightened awareness.

The person living in a high vibrational state is not judgemental or fault finding. They accept others for who or what they are and allow them to be. They do not spend time watching violent TV shows or pay much attention to constant negative broadcasts via the media.

It is because of this high vibrational state that the person who is "connected" with the field will attract the same back into their lives with ease. Therefore, the connected are not surprised by the arrival of success or abundance. They know in their hearts that those seemingly positive happenings were brought into their lives because they were already connected with them.

People resonating on a high vibration will light up the room and shine their light on everyone they come into contact with. They love to inspire others and the level of their energy is exceptionally high. They have understood that thoughts, emotions and feelings are vibrations and that the frequency of these vibrations can create disturbances, not only in ourselves, but in everything that is made up of the same material.

Living life connected and nurtured by the infinite loving and giving Universe is a magical and wonderful way to live.

This can be you.

Every time you change your state of being and begin your

day by opening your heart to the elevated states that connect you to a love for life and a state of gratitude, you are already connected.

All you need to do is give yourself permission to say, 'Yes'.